250+ RECIPES FOR THE FRUIT JUICER THIS BOOK CONTAINS JUST THE BEST JUICING RECIPES

DION J. SMITH

TABLEOFCONTENTS

NUTRIBULLET RECIPE BOOK 1

TABLEOFCONTENTS 2

INTRODUCTION 30

RECIPES 34

    1. Breakfast Smoothie 34
    2. Back to the Basics 35
    3. Protein Breakfast Smoothie 37
    4. Super Antioxidant Smoothie 38
    5. NutriBullet Chimichurri Sauce 39
    6. Pick-Me-Up Smoothie 40
    7. Nutribullet iced coffee recipe 42
    8. Apple and Cinnamon Nutribullet Smoothie Recipe 43
    9. Make the Easiest & Yummiest 4-Ingredient Strawberry Banana Smoothie 44
    10. Nutribullet Recipe: Frozen Summer Berries Smoothie 45
    11. Pineapple Ginger Immunity Smoothie 46
    12. Nutribullet Pancakes 47
    13. Three Ingredient Green Smoothie 48
    14. Mood-Boosting Nutribullet Smoothie Recipe 49
    15. Cleansing Smoothie Recipe with Ginger and Apple Cider Vinegar 50
    16. NUTRIBULLET PINK DETOX BLAST SMOOTHIE RECIPE 51
    17. Orange Juice in a Blender (Featuring the Nutribullet) 51
    18. Farm Fresh Tomato Basil Soup 52
    19. Healthy Smooth Peanut Butter 53
    20. Apple Pie Smoothie 54
    21. Healthy Green Juice 55
    22. NutriBullet Skinny Blast Smoothie 57
    23. Melon-Berry Milkshake 58
    24. NutriBullet Frozen Strawberry Daiquiri 59
    25. Low Sugar Avocado Blueberry Smoothie 60
    26. GREEN POWER SMOOTHIE + NUTRIBULLET GIVEAWAY 62
    27. Creamy Cauliflower Comfort Soup (recipe from the NutriBullet Balance App) 63

28. Nutribullet Six-Second Milkshake Recipe 64
29. Greek Frappe 66
30. How to Make Mustard in the Nutribullet 67
31. Banana, Blueberry & Seeds Smoothie 68
32. Nutribullet guacamole 69
33. Black Forest Smoothie 70
34. Easy Cheesy Blender Scrambled Eggs 70
35. LOW-CALORIE NUTRIBULLET SMOOTHIE 71
36. Black Forest Smoothie 72
37. The Best Breakfast Smoothie 74
38. 6 Healthy Superfood Smoothies 74
39. How to Make the Ultimate Healthy Breakfast Smoothie 78
40. 5 High Protein Fruit Smoothie Recipes For Weight Loss (5 Ingredients or Less!) 79
41. Oatmeal Smoothie 84
42. GREEN PROTEIN POWER BREAKFAST SMOOTHIE 86
43. Peanut Butter Banana Smoothie 87
44. Peanut Butter Banana Smoothie 88
45. How to Make a Perfect Green Smoothie 88
46. Healthy Breakfast Smoothie BERRY 90
47. winter breakfast smoothie 91
48. Simple Green Smoothie 92
49. HEALTHY BREAKFAST SMOOTHIE – GLUTEN-FREE & VEGAN 93
50. GREEN BREAKFAST SMOOTHIE 95
51. banana oat breakfast smoothie 96
52. High Fiber Smoothie 97
53. Banana Oatmeal Breakfast Smoothie 98
54. Breakfast Energy Smoothie 99
55. Creamsicle Breakfast Smoothie 100
56. My Favorite Green Smoothie 101
57. PEVEY CRUMBLE SHAKE & 19 MORE VEGAN SMOOTHIES 102
58. Breakfast Energy Smoothie 103
59. Berry Breakfast Smoothie 104
60. HEALTHY OATMEAL SMOOTHIE 104
61. Power Breakfast Smoothie 106
62. Strawberry Sunrise Breakfast Smoothie 107
63. SUNRISE BREAKFAST SMOOTHIE 108
64. Peveryes and Cream Oatmeal Breakfast Smoothie 109

65. Green Breakfast Smoothie 110
66. Beet Banana Breakfast Smoothie 111
67. Cereal Milk Breakfast Smoothie (3 Ways!) 112
68. CINNAMON ROLL BREAKFAST SMOOTHIE 113
69. Clean Eating Breakfast Smoothie 114
70. Frozen fruit smoothies 115
71. Mango Smoothie 116
72. MAKE-AHEAD SMOOTHIES 117
73. BEST GREEN JUICE 118
74. METABOLISM, BALANCED MEAL, GREAT FOR HAIR, SKIN, AND NAILS} 118
75. Apple Cobbler Smoothie 120
76. Apple a Day 122
77. Apple Pie Smoothie 123
78. Apple Pear Ginger Smoothie 124
79. Santa Barbara Tropical Ginger Smoothie Recipe 125
80. Tropical Ginger Smoothie 126
81. Tropical Green Smoothie 127
82. Tropical Mango Pineapple Smoothie 128
83. Tropical Tumeric Ginger Smoothie 129
84. Tropical Carrot Juice 130
85. The Best Detox Green Smoothie Recipe 131
86. Ginger Matcha Smoothie Bowl 132
87. Smoothies 101: A pediatrician's prescription 133
88. Golden Milk Tropical Turmeric Smoothie 135
89. The Cheeky Monkey Smoothie 136
90. Easy Delicious Tropical Green Smoothie 137
91. Tropical Green Flaxseed Smoothie 138
92. Sunshine Smoothie Bowl 139
93. Sweet Ginger Basil Smoothie 140
94. VANILLA MANGO SPINACH SMOOTHIE 141
95. Sunshine Tropical Smoothie with Turmeric 142
96. Vegan Tropical Butternut Squash Smoothie 143
97. Immune Booster Sweet Green Smoothie 144
98. GREEN APPLE LEMON CUCUMBER GINGER SMOOTHIE 145
100. Tropical Fruit Smoothie with Coconut Flour 147
101. Carrot Apple Ginger Smoothie 148
102. WATCH HOW TO MAKE COFFEE SMOOTHIE 149

103. PERCENT DAILY VALUES ARe based on a 2000 calorie diet. 151
104. Coffee Smoothie | Healthy Blended Coffee! 153
105. Creamy Coffee & Banana Smoothie 154
106. Coffee Protein Smoothie 155
107. Healthy Protein Coffee Smoothie...157
108. Coffee Smoothie with Banana and Oats..159
109. Loaded Coffee Smoothie 160
110. Coffee Protein Shake Recipe 161
111. MOCHA COFFEE SMOOTHIE 163
112. Iced Coffee Smoothie 164
113. Peanut Butter Coffee Smoothie 165
114. Competitive Coffee Smoothie with Dates & Banana.....................167
115. I'm ready to make my smoothie..168
116. KETO COFFEE SMOOTHIE 169
117. HEALTHY CHOCOLATE COFFEE SMOOTHIE..................................171
118. This healthy Chocolate Coffee Protein Smoothie.........................171
119. Cold Brew Coffee Banana Smoothie..173
120. Blueberry Coffee Breakfast Smoothie 175
121. Easy Banana Spinach Smoothie 179
122. GREEN PROTEIN POWER BREAKFAST SMOOTHIE 180
123. Creamy, Coffee Protein Smoothie 181
124. Summerlicious fruit smoothies...182
125. Energizing Green Smoothie 186
126. BULLETPROOF COFFEE RECIPE 187
127. CHOCOLATE ALMOND COFFEE SMOOTHIE 188
128. BASIC GREEN SMOOTHIE RECIPE...189
129. Perfect Celery Smoothie...190
130. RED BEET SMOOTHIE..191
131. Strawberry Banana Smoothie {made with Almond Breeze}..........192
132. Coffee Protein Shake 193
133. STRAWBERRY BANANA SMOOTHIE RECIPE......................................194
134. 3 Ingredient strawberry banana smoothie......................................195
135. THE BEST STRAWBERRY BANANA SMOOTHIE 196
136. Greek Yogurt Smoothie 197
137. KISS Strawberry Banana Lemon Smoothie 199
138. High Fiber Smoothie 200
139. Peveryes & Cream Oatmeal Smoothie 201
140. High Fiber Fruit and Veggie Smoothie..202

141. Broccoli Smoothie 203
142. AVOCADO PINEAPPLE HIGH FIBER SMOOTHIE 203
143. The Best Low Carb Green Smoothie 204
144. Ultra-Satisfying Strawberry Banana Smoothie Recipe 205
145. APPLE-BERRY COLLAGEN SMOOTHIE 206
146. CHOCOLATE FIBER SMOOTHIE CUBES 207
147. DETOX GREEN SMOOTHIE 208
148. High-Fiber Kale and Apple Detox Smoothie for Healthy Digestion 209
149. Slimming Green Smoothie 210
150. High Fiber Blueberry Kale Smoothie 211
151. MIXED BERRY SMOOTHIE 212
152. Five-Ingredient Go-To Green Smoothie 213
153. EVERY BANANA FLAX SMOOTHIE 214
154. 3-INGREDIENT BERRY SMOOTHIE 215
155. 3 Veggie-Packed Smoothies for Beginners 216
156. Glowing Green Smoothie 217
157. Banana Spinach Smoothie 218
158. HEALTHY RED AND GREEN SMOOTHIE 219
159. Alkaline Smoothie 221
160. Carrot Ginger Turmeric Smoothie 223
161. ANTIOXIDANT-RICH BLUEBERRY SMOOTHIE 225
162. Keto Low Carb Smoothie With Almond Milk 226
163. Apple Pomegranate Smoothie Bowl Recipe 227
BLEND THE APPLE, POMEGRANATE SEEDS, OATS, PEANUT BUTTER, AND MILK IN A BLENDER. 227
164. Harley Pasternak Breakfast Smoothie 228
165. The Ultimate Lactation Smoothie Recipe 229
166. Carrot Beetroot Juice with Apples and Celery 231
167. Coconut Water Smoothie 232
168. HEALTHY GREEN SMOOTHIE 233
169. BEST TURMERIC SMOOTHIE 235
170. PEAR AND CINNAMON SMOOTHIE (DAIRY-FREE) 236
171. Zucchini Smoothie Recipe 237
172. Watermelon Strawberry Smoothie 239
173. Strawberry Banana Oat Smoothie 240
174. Immunity Boosting Smoothie Recipe 241
In a high-powered blender, combine all ingredients in the order stated (sweetener is optional); blend until smooth. 241

175. Cashew Apple Green Smoothie 242
176. Greek Frappe 244
177. Easy Greek Frappe Recipe 245
178. DALGONA WHIPPED COFFEE VS THE GREEK FRAPPE 246
179. How to make frappe – Greek iced coffee 247
180. DALTON COFFEE VS GREEK FRAPPE 248
181. Greek Iced Coffee 249
182. Nescafe Frappe 250
183. Matcha Frappe 250
184. NUTRIBULLET BEAUTY BLAST SMOOTHIE RECIPE 252
185. GRAPE JUICE FRESHLY MADE 253
186. ROASTED STRAWBERRY PROTEIN SMOOTHIE 254
187. In a medium bowl, Carrot Orange Banana Smoothies 255
188. Delicious Mung Bean Sprouts Juice & Smoothie Recipe 256
189. CREAMY CAULIFLOWER SOUP 257
190. Creamy Cauliflower Comfort Soup 258
191. CREAMY CAULIFLOWER & POTATO SOUP 259
192. CREAMY CAULIFLOWER WILD RICE SOUP 261
193. Immunity Blast Smoothie 263
194. Fresh Lemon Ginger Detoxifying Smoothie 265
195. Berry Blast Smoothies 265
196. Berry Crunch Smoothie Bowl 266
196. Berry Dragon Fruit Smoothie 267
197. Perfect Dragon Fruit Smoothie 269
198. Creamy Dragon Fruit Smoothie Bowl 270
199. Dragon Fruit (Pitaya) Smoothie Bowl 273
200. Pink Pitaya Protein Smoothie 274
201. Dragon Fruit And Yogurt Smoothie Recipe 275
202. Dragon fruit Mango Smoothie 276
203. Dragon Fruit Blackberry Smoothie 277
204. Dragon Fruit Chia Coconut Pudding Smoothie 278
205. Raspberry Coconut Dragon Fruit Smoothie Bowls 280
206. Dragon fruit and a pinch of honey 281
207. DAIRY-FREE DRAGONFRUIT SMOOTHIE BOWL 282
208. Almond Banana Dragon Fruit Bowl 283
209. Healthy Dragon Fruit Smoothie 285
210. Triple Cherry Berry Watermelon Smoothie 287
211. Blueberry Watermelon Smoothie Recipe 288

212. Watermelon Raspberry Smoothie 289
213. Paleo Watermelon Berry Smoothie 290
214. Vegan + GF 291
215. Clean Eating Triple Berry Watermelon Smoothie 292
216. Strawberry Watermelon Smoothie 293
217. Watermelon Berry Kale Smoothie 295
218. Watermelon Raspberry Mint Smoothie 296
220. Melon-Berry Milkshake 297
221. Refreshing Summer Smoothie Recipe 298
222. TRIPLE BERRY BANANA SMOOTHIE RECIPE 300
223. Peanut Butter Blueberry Banana Smoothie 301
224. Peanut Butter Blueberry Banana Smoothie 302
226. No Banana Berry Smoothie Bowl (vegan) 304
227. Must-try Fruit Smoothie with Silken Tofu and Peanut Butter 305
228. SPINACH BLUEBERRY AND BANANA SMOOTHIE 306
229. Blueberry Cheesecake Smoothie 307
231. Vega Blueberry Vanilla Smoothie 307
232. Chocolate Banana Protein Smoothie 308
233. Dairy-Free Mango Colada Smoothies or Smoothie Bowls 309
234. Mango Basil Colada Recipe 311
235. mango piña colada cocktail 312
236. Skinny Mango Colada With (Optional) Jalapeños 313
237. Mango Colada with banana and grapefruit 315
238. Carnival Cruise Lines' Mango Colada Recipe 316
239. Mango Sunrise Piña Colada 317
240. Mango Castaway 318
241. Blueberry-Mango Colada Salad 319
242. Pomegranate Mango Colada Popsicles 320
243. Recipe: Bacardi Mango Coladas 323
244. Digestive Smoothie 325
245. Pineapple Ginger Tummy Soothing Smoothie 325
246. SMOOTHIE FOR BLOATING 327
247. Digestive aid detox smoothie (pineapple, ginger & mint) 328
248. HEALTHY GUT VANILLA CHAI SMOOTHIE 329
249. Preparation: 5 min 330
250. Happy Gut Kefir Smoothie 331
251. flight therapy green smoothie 332
252. Tropical Papaya Pineapple Kale Green Smoothie Recipe 333

253. Tropical Melon Smoothie 334
254. emergency super smoothie 335
255. DOWN-REGULATION IVF SMOOTHIE 336
256. Apple Pie Smoothie 338
257. Anti-Inflammatory Blueberry Smoothie 340
258. Whole 30 Matcha Smoothie 341
259. SMOOTHIE MADE WITH NUTRIBULLET. 342
260. NutriBullet Smoothie Recipe Featuring Pomegranate Seeds 343
261. Banana Almond Mocha Smoothie 344
262. Peanut Butter Espresso Smoothie 346
263. Genuine Greek Frappe 347
264. Frozen Tropical Colada 348
265. Pineapple Mango Pina Colada 349
266. Almond Coffee Green Smoothie 350
267. BASIC SMOOTHIE RECIPE 351

THE END **353**

INTRODUCTION

FOR NUTRIBULLET FANS, THIS IS THE ULTIMATE GUIDE. MORE THAN 250 RECIPES ARE AVAILABLE FOR: - SMOOTHIES WITH DELECTABLE SUPERFOODS

What Makes Your Recipes So Special?

You can do the following using my specifically formulated recipes:

Obtain optimum health

Have an abundance of energy and vitality.

Get to your optimum weight and keep it there.

It would help if you were glowing.

Enjoy a long and healthy life.

My recipes always include nutritional information and have all of the dietary aspects you seek (except the occasional naughty day with a higher calorie count!):

Low-fat diet

calorie-free

Sugar-free

Fiber-rich

Are they inexpensive and straightforward to make?

Are nice and delectable

Provide quick results

Adapt to a fast-paced lifestyle

The motivation to maintain your new healthy lifestyle may weaken, and old unhealthy habits may resurface. As a result, I've created these recipes to help you sustain your passion.

What Can You Tell Me About Your Book?

Heart Health: Heart disease is responsible for one out of every four deaths in the United States.

Radiant Skin: If you have glowing skin, you will exude health and confidence, attracting attention from the opposite sex and at work.

Energy Boost: One out of every ten persons suffers from chronic fatigue.

Superfoods: This category is for folks who wish to give their bodies a concentrated boost of all the vitamins and nutrients they require.

I'm sure you're drooling at the prospect of satisfying your taste senses and infusing your body with all the goodness that nature has to offer. Here's a tiny sample to whet your appetite:

Smoothie with Chia Seeds from the Rainforest

Smoothie with berries for breakfast

Smoothie for a Flat Stomach

Smoothie for Younger-Looking Skin

Smoothie with Shamrocks

Smoothie with Antioxidants and Anti-Aging Ingredients

Smoothie with raw mint and chocolate

Smoothie with Bananarama

If you don't have all of the ingredients for the recipes, don't worry. Components can be substituted or omitted. The critical point is that you are providing your body with all of nature's goodness.

Today, we decide to live a longer, healthier, and happier life—a life with more energy, time, and weight loss. Your new brilliance and self-assurance are waiting for you.

Scroll to the top of the page and download your copy right away to start reaping the rewards!

RECIPES

1. BREAKFAST SMOOTHIE

Ingredients

- 1 cups of spinach
- ½ Banana, frozen
- 1 1/2 cup of Almond Milk, vanilla, unsweetened
- 1/4 cup ofgluten-free
- Oats, rolled,
- One tbsp peanut Butter, creamy, unsalted
- 1 tbspHoney

Directions

1. Blend the ingredients in the order stated until smooth.
2. Have fun!

Nutritional information

Recipe: Breakfast Smoothie

Serving in this recipe: 1

Calories: 346.6

Total Fat: 14.3 g 22%

Saturated Fat: 1.9 g   9.7%

Cholesterol: 0 mg   0%

Sodium: 268.9 mg   11.2%

Total Carbs: 49.5 g   16.5%

Dietary Fiber: 6.2 g   24.9%

Sugar: 25.1 g

Protein: 9.2 g   18.3%

Vitamin A: 11.9%   Vitamin C: 21.1%

Calcium: 8.8%   Iron: 15%

2. BACK TO THE BASICS

Ingredients

- 1 cups of spinach
- 1/2 cup of Blueberries
- 1/2 cups of strawberries
- 1/2 Banana
- 1 1/2 cup of Coconut Water
- 1 tbsp Hemp Seeds

Directions

1. Blend the ingredients in the order stated until smooth.
2. Have fun!

Nutritional information

Recipe: Back to the Basics

Serving in this recipe: 1

Calories: 246.2

Total Fat: 5.7 g   8.7%

Saturated Fat: 0.6 g   2.9%

Cholesterol: 0 mg   0%

3. PROTEIN BREAKFAST SMOOTHIE

Ingredients

- 2 cups of spinach
- 1/2 Banana
- 1 1/2 cup of almond milk, unsweetened
- 1/2 cup of greek yogurt, plain, non-fat
- One tbsp peanut Butter, creamy, unsalted

- One tbspSuperfood Essential Vanilla Plant-Based Protein
- 1/2 tspCinnamon, ground

Directions

1. Blend the ingredients in the order stated until smooth.
2. Have fun!
3. Enjoy!

Nutritional information

Recipe: Protein Breakfast Smoothie

Serving in this recipe: 1

Calories: 322.7

Total Fat: 13.4 g 20.6%

Saturated Fat: 2.2 g   11%

Cholesterol: 6.5 mg   2.2%

Sodium: 403.2 mg   16.8%

Total Carbs: 31 g10.3%

4.SUPER ANTIOXIDANT SMOOTHIE

INGREDIENTS

- Eight flOuncesAlmond Milk
- 1 cup of kale
- ½ cup of Blueberries
- ½ cup of Purple Grapes
- ½ cup of shredded carrots
- 10 Almonds

INSTRUCTIONS

1. In a Nutribullet cup, mix all of the ingredients.

2. Fill the container with fresh almond milk till it reaches the maximum fill line.
3. Blend everything until it's smooth and uniform.

Nutrition Information:

Amount Per Serving: CALORIES: 226TOTAL FAT: 9gSATURATED FAT: 0.5gTRANS FAT: 0gCHOLESTEROL: 0mgSODIUM: 187mgCARBOHYDRATES: 34gFIBER: 6gSUGAR: 23gPROTEIN:

5.NUTRIBULLET CHIMICHURRI SAUCE

Total: 5 min

Active: 5 min

Ingredients

- 1/2 cup of fresh cilantro leaves
- 1/2 cup of fresh flat-leaf parsley leaves
- 3 tbsp red wine vinegar
- 1/2 tsp crushed red pepper flakes
- Three cloves garlic
- Kosher salt
- 1/4 cup of olive oil

Directions

1. In a NutriBullet short cup of water, mix the cilantro, parsley, vinegar, red pepper flakes, garlic, and 1 teaspoon salt (18 ounces). Blend until the extractor blade is attached and the mixture is chopped, scraping down the sides as needed. Pulse in the olive oil until it's barely combined. Use right away.

6.PICK-ME-UP SMOOTHIE

Prep Time:5 minutes

Total Time:5 minutes

Ingredients

- 1 cup of spinach
- ½ small cucumber
- ½ celery stalk
- 1 tsp. gingerroot
- 1 tsp. parsley
- 2 tsp. lemon juice
- Five mint leaves
- 1 cup of water
- 1 cup of ice

Instructions

2. Following the directions on the Nutribullet Balance app, add the ingredients one by one.
3. Forty-five seconds of blending (the app will time it for you).
4. Stir with a spoon or a celery stalk in a glass.

Nutrition Facts

Pick-Me-Up Smoothie

Amount Per Serving

Calories 33

% Daily Value*

Sodium 52mg2%

Carbohydrates 8g3%

Fiber 2g8%

Sugar 2g2%

Protein 2g4%

Vitamin A 500IU10%

Vitamin C 24.8mg30%

Calcium 80mg8%

Iron 0.9mg5%

Net carbs 6g

* Percent Daily Values are based on a 2000 calorie diet.

7. NUTRIBULLET ICED COFFEE RECIPE

Prep Time 5 minutes

Total Time 5 minutes

Ingredients

- 2 tsp instant coffee
- 2 tsp granulated sweetener
- 50 ml hot water
- 50 ml cold water
- 200 ml cold milk
- lots of ice
- Monin chocolate mint syrup or any syrup of your choice

Instructions

1. Add the instant coffee, granulated sweetener, hot water, then cold water in that order.
2. With a spoon, stir the mixture. There were still a few coffee granules after a few seconds, but I didn't bother about them.
3. I blitzed it in my Nutribullet for a few seconds once it had cooled. It's best not to use the Nutribullet with hot liquids because the vapor can be harmful. By ignoring this, I may have almost slashed my face open!
4. Pour in the cold water and ice. After that, blitz in a Nutribullet.
5. Drizzle a little Monin chocolate mint syrup around the rim of a glass. You may use any flavor syrup you want, and there are lots of choices!

8. APPLE AND CINNAMON NUTRIBULLET SMOOTHIE RECIPE

INGREDIENTS

- One handful spinach
- One apple

- 1tsp cinnamon
- 1tsp vanilla
- ½tsp nutmeg
- One handful almonds
- ½cup of almond milk
- coconut water, to the max line
- 1tsp vanilla

METHOD

Fill the Nutribullet's tall cup halfway with coconut water and add all of the solid ingredients. Blend for around 30 seconds, or until smooth.

9.MAKE THE EASIEST & YUMMIEST 4-INGREDIENT STRAWBERRY BANANA SMOOTHIE

INGREDIENTS

- 1 cup of almond milk
- 1/2 cup of Greek yogurt
- 6-7 large strawberries
- One banana
- 1/2 cup of ice
- whipped cream (optional)

DIRECTIONS

1. Blend the almond milk and yogurt first, then the fruit and ice in a blender (I used a Nutribullet).
2. Blend for 40 seconds, or until the drink is smooth and the ice has entirely dissolved.
3. Top with whipped cream and pour into a glass. That concludes our discussion. Take pleasure in it!

10.NUTRIBULLET RECIPE: FROZEN SUMMER BERRIES SMOOTHIE

PREP TIME:1 min

COOK TIME:2 mins

TOTAL TIME:3 mins

INGREDIENTS

- 150 g Frozen Berries.
- For this version, my berries were raspberries, blackberries, blackcurrants, and redcurrants.
- 450 ml Unsweetened Almond Milk, although you could substitute other milk.

INSTRUCTIONS

1. Place the berries in the Nutribullet cup while they are still frozen.
2. Blast for a minute with the milk, then rest for a minute before blasting for another minute.
3. Serve and have fun.

11.PINEAPPLE GINGER IMMUNITY SMOOTHIE

prep time: 5 MINUTES

total time: 5 MINUTES

INGREDIENTS

- 4 Tbsp frozen pineapple
- 1/2 cup of baby carrots
- 1 tsp ground turmeric
- 1 tsp ground ginger
- 1/2 lemon, peeled
- 1/2 orange, peeled
- 3 tsp hemp seeds
- 1 cup of Ice
- 1 cup of water

INSTRUCTIONS

1. Add the pineapple, baby carrots, turmeric, ginger, lemon, orange, hemp seeds, ice, and water to the nutribullet balancing container. Place the lid on the pan and flip it over.

2. Blend for 45 seconds or until completely smooth.
3. Top with more pineapple chunks and hemp seeds if desired.

Nutrition Information

Amount Per Serving

Calories 162

Total Fat 5g

Sodium 60mg

Fiber 6g

Sugar 20g

Protein 4g

12. NUTRIBULLET PANCAKES

Prep Time 5 minutes

Cook Time 3 minutes

Ingredients

- 225 g plain flour
- 1 tbsp baking powder
- 1 tsp sugar
- ½ tsp vanilla extract
- pinch salt
- Two large eggs
- 30 g melted butter

Instructions

1. There isn't much to this that is difficult! Simply combine all of the ingredients in a nutribullet and blend until smooth. It's that easy!
2. Place lumps of the mixture in a heated frying pan and cook for a minute on one side or until bubbles begin to form.
3. Cook for another 30 seconds on the opposite side, or until both sides are brown.

4. Serve warm with your favorite toppings. My daughters enjoy the chocolate spread, strawberries, and bananas, while I want maple syrup. Take pleasure in it!

13. THREE INGREDIENT GREEN SMOOTHIE

INGREDIENTS

- One cup of spinach
- Two stalks of celery trimmed and cut into small pieces
- 1/4 cup of natural unsweetened applesauce
- 2-4 tbsp cold water depending on desired texture
- 1-2 ice cubes

INSTRUCTIONS

1. In a NutriBullet, blender, or food processor, puree the spinach and celery for 30-45 seconds or until no large chunks appear.
2. Blend the applesauce, ice, and water until the drink is smooth Serve and enjoy!

14. MOOD-BOOSTING ÑUTRIBULLET SMOOTHIE RECIPE

INGREDIENTS

- 50g banana, chopped
- 100g pineapple chunks
- 1tbsp oats
- 1tsp coconut oil
- ¼tsp cinnamon
- almond milk or milk, to the line

METHOD

1. In the Nutribullet, combine the diced banana, pineapple pieces, oats, coconut oil, and cinnamon.
2. Almond milk to the top.
3. Blitz until a smooth consistency is achieved.

15. CLEANSING SMOOTHIE RECIPE WITH GINGER AND APPLE CIDER VINEGAR

PREP TIME: 5 mins

TOTAL TIME: 5 mins

INGREDIENTS

- 1/2 Cup frozen veggies
- 1/2 Cup chopped apple
- 1/4 a frozen banana
- One celery stick
- juice from half lemon
- 1 tsp apple cider vinegar
- 1 TBSP chia seeds
- about 1/2 tsp fresh chopped ginger
- filtered water to the fill line about a cup of

INSTRUCTIONS

1. Blend all of the ingredients in the NutriBullet. As needed, add extra water. To add some sweetness, sprinkle with chocolate nibs.

16. NUTRIBULLET PINK DETOX BLAST SMOOTHIE RECIPE

INGREDIENTS

- ½ cup of apple
- ½ cup of avocado
- ½ cup of beets
- ½ cup of celery
- 1 cup of strawberries, frozen
- 2 tbsp lemon juice
- 1 cup of coconut water
- ½ cup of ice
- Detox & Cleanse Boost (optional)

INSTRUCTIONS

2. Fill a blender halfway with water, add the ingredients, and blend until a smooth consistency is reached.

17. ORANGE JUICE IN A BLENDER (FEATURING THE NUTRIBULLET)

Prep Time 3 mins

Total Time 3 min

Ingredients

- 2 Oranges peeled and broken into smaller pieces
- 1 Water Enough to cover orange in the blender.

Instructions

3. Take the peels from the oranges and place them in the blender. You can use as many oranges as you want, as long as there are enough to create a vortex inside the blender pint glass.

18. FARM FRESH TOMATO BASIL SOUP

Prep Time: 5 minutes

Cook Time: 30 minutes

Ingredients

- 4 Roma tomatoes
- 4 cups of tomato juice
- 15 fresh basil leaves
- 2 tsp garlic, minced
- 1 tbsp extra virgin olive oil
- optional - salt and pepper, as need

Instructions

4. Roma tomatoes should be cored, sliced in half, and added to NutriBullet Select.
5. Toss in some basil leaves.
6. After 5 seconds of pulsing, blend until the ingredients are smooth.
7. In a blender, combine the garlic, olive oil, and tomato juice.
8. Blend until the mixture is completely smooth.
9. Pour into soup bowls and top with croutons for a refreshing summer soup.

Notes

If you prefer a creamy tomato basil soup: After the soup is finished simmering for 30 minutes, add 1 cup of heavy whipping cream. Stir and simmer for 10 minutes. Remove soup from heat, serve and enjoy!

19. HEALTHY SMOOTH PEANUT BUTTER

PREP TIME 1 min

TOTAL TIME 1 min

INGREDIENTS

- 1 cup of peanuts
- 1 tbsp peanut oil
- 1 tsp honey (optional)
- 1/4 tsp salt (optional)

INSTRUCTIONS

1.
2. In a sizeable NutriBullet container, combine all of the ingredients. Attach the extractor blade attachment and blend for 5 seconds, or until a doughy substance forms and adheres to the container's walls. The blades will not be touching the peanut mixture at this time, and the sound will change.
3. Scrape the peanut dough from the sides of the container. Put the cap, set the container on the base, blend for 10 seconds or until the peanut butter is completely smooth.
4. Place the peanut butter in a sterile container and keep it at room temperature or in the refrigerator.

20. APPLE PIE SMOOTHIE

Prep Time 2 minutes

Cook Time 1 minute

Total Time 3 minutes

Ingredients

- 1 Apple
- 1 Banana
- 1 Scoop Protein Powder Vanilla
- 1 tsp vanilla if no vanilla protein powder
- 1 Tbsp chia seeds optional
- A dash of cinnamon
- Milk to fill the container Can use nut milk or soy milk

Instructions

1. Blend the ingredients in a Nutribullet until smooth. Typically, around 30 seconds is all that is required.

21. HEALTHY GREEN JUICE

Prep Time 5 mins

Total Time 5 mins

Ingredients

- Large handful of Kale
- 1/2 bunch of parsley
- 1/2 cucumber
- Two celery stalks
- 1/2 Granny Smith apple
- 1/2 to 3/4 cup of seedless green grapes are not cut up

Instructions

2. In a food processor/extractor, combine all of the ingredients. (I used a Nutri-Bullet to make this.)
3. Run until entirely blended, around 20-30 seconds in a Nutri-bullet.
4. If your juice isn't sweet enough, add different grapes or 1/2 a banana to sweeten it up.
5. Serve with ice cubes.

22. NUTRIBULLET SKINNY BLAST SMOOTHIE

PREP: 5 MIN

COOK:1 MIN

TOTAL:6 MIN

INGREDIENTS

- One banana sliced
- One carrot
- One orange peeled
- 2 cups of spinach
- 1 tbsp hemp seeds
- 1 tbsp pumpkin seeds
- 1/2 cup of water
- 1 cup of ice

INSTRUCTIONS

1. Place ingredients into a blender, fill to the max water line and blend until a smooth consistency is achieved.

23. MELON-BERRY MILKSHAKE

PREP TIME5 minutes

COOK TIME5 minutes

TOTAL TIME10 minutes

INGREDIENTS

- Two wedges of fresh cantaloupe, cut into chunks (about ¼ large melon)
- 1 cup of fresh or frozen blueberries
- 1 tbsp chia seeds
- About ½ cup of unsweetened plain almond milk (to fill line)

INSTRUCTIONS

Place everything into the NutriBullet and blend until smooth. Makes 2 servings.

Nutrition Information:

Amount Per Serving: CALORIES: 117TOTAL FAT: 3.5gCHOLESTEROL: 0mgSODIUM: 81mgFIBER: 5.6gSUGAR: 15.6gPROTEIN: 3.3g

24. NUTRIBULLET FROZEN STRAWBERRY DAIQUIRI

Total: 5 min

Active: 5 min

Ingredients

- 2 cups of frozen strawberries (about 12 ounces)
- 1/3 cup of fresh lime juice
- 1/3 cup of light agave syrup
- 3 ounces white rum

Directions

2. A NutriBullet blender is required.
3. In a NutriBullet tall cup of water, mix the strawberries, lime juice, agave, and rum (24 ounces). Blend with the extractor blade until smooth and combined. Serve right away.

25. LOW SUGAR AVOCADO BLUEBERRY SMOOTHIE

prep time: 5 MINUTES

cook time: 0 MINUTES

total time: 5 MINUTES

Ingredients

- 1 cup of frozen blueberries
- 1/2 cup of ice cubes
- 1/2 cup of almond milk
- 1/2 cup of chopped frozen cauliflower
- 1/4 avocado (about 3 tbsp)
- 1 tbsp hemp seeds

Instructions

In a NutriBullet or blender, combine all of the ingredients and blend until smooth.

If desired, pour into a glass or bowl and top with more chia seeds!

Nutrition Facts

Serves 1

Amount Per Serving

Calories 287

% Daily Value*

Total Fat 14.7g   23%

Cholesterol 0g   0%

Sodium 112.4mg   5%

Total Carbohydrate 33.6g   11%

Dietary Fiber 13.5g   54%

Sugars 16.3g

Protein 10.5g   21%

Vitamin A1%Vitamin C82%

26. GREEN POWER SMOOTHIE + NUTRIBULLET GIVEAWAY

Prep Time: 5 mins

Total Time: 5 mins

INGREDIENTS

- Three ripe kiwifruits
- One ripe banana
- 20 mint leaves

- One handful of spinach leaves
- 1/2 lime, juiced
- Two dates
- 1/2 cup of water
- 1 tsp moringa powder (optional)
- 1 tsp matcha powder (optional)
- 1/2 tsp spirulina powder (optional)

INSTRUCTIONS

1. Place all ingredients in a blender and puree until completely smooth. Serve immediately. Enjoy!

27. CREAMY CAULIFLOWER COMFORT SOUP (RECIPE FROM THE NUTRIBULLET BALANCE APP)

Prep Time 10 mins

Total Time 10 mins

Ingredients

- 2 cups of cauliflower, steamed and chopped
- 2 cups of almond milk (unsweetened)
- ¼ tsp garlic powder
- ¼ tsp salt
- ¼ tsp black pepper
- US Customary - Metric

Instructions

2. Place all ingredients in a blender and blend until smooth.

Nutrition Facts

Calories 67 Calories from Fat 36

% Daily Value*

Fat 4g 6%

Sodium 648mg 28%

Potassium 319mg 9%

Carbohydrates 6g2%

Fiber 3g13%

Sugar 3g3%

Calcium 324mg32%

Iron 0.5mg3%

28. NUTRIBULLET SIX-SECOND MILKSHAKE RECIPE
Ingredients
- Milk: 1 cup of
- Vanilla Ice-Cream: 1 ½ cup of
- Chocolate Syrup: ½ cup of

Method
3. The sole step in producing this straightforward and time-saving recipe is to blitz all of the ingredients combined in a mixer until it reaches a dense and creamy consistency with no lumps. If you want your milkshake to be thinner, just add more milk while keeping the other ingredients the same. However, if you want a thicker milkshake, double the amount of vanilla ice cream while keeping the rest of the elements the same.
4. Fill a glass with it and serve. You can even add a bit of chocolate syrup on top.
5. You can also make a Blueberry Milkshake by replacing the chocolate syrup with frozen berries. Then, add colored chocolate candy to the average Milkshake Recipe to make a Bullet Blizzard.

29. GREEK FRAPPE

TOTAL TIME3 mins

INGREDIENTS
- 1 tsp instant coffee only instant coffee will work
- 1 tsp sugar, xylitol,
- 1 cup of water room temperature
- splash of milk of choice optional

INSTRUCTIONS

1. In your Nutribullet, blitz the instant coffee, sugar/sweetener, and water for around 20 seconds, or until incredibly frothy.
2. Pour your Frappe into a tall glass with a splash of milk (don't try to add your milk before blitzing).
3. That concludes our discussion. Take pleasure in it.

30. HOW TO MAKE MUSTARD IN THE NUTRIBULLET

Ingredients

1 1/4 cup of white wine vinegar

1/2 cup of yellow mustard seeds

1/2 cup of brown mustard seeds

1 1/2-2 tsp sea salt

1 tsp ground turmeric

1/4 tsp ground allspice

1/4 tsp ground cinnamon

1/4 tsp ground ginger

dash of nutmeg

water (if needed)

Instructions

1. IN A 4-CUP PYREX DISH, STIR TOGETHER THE VINEGAR AND MUSTARD SEEDS, COVER, AND SET ASIDE FOR 1 DAY AT ROOM TEMPERATURE. Then, TO KEEP LIGHT OUT, DRAPE A TOWEL OVER IT OR STORE IT IN A CABINET.
2. Fill a tall Nutribullet cup with soaked mustard seeds and vinegar the next day. Sea salt, turmeric, allspice, cinnamon, ginger, and nutmeg

are all good additions. Blend until smooth, adding water 1-2 tbsp at a time if necessary to reach the desired consistency.

3. Place in a 16-ounce mason jar, cover, and refrigerate for 2-4 days before using.

31. BANANA, BLUEBERRY & SEEDS SMOOTHIE

INGREDIENTS

- 1 tbsp sunflower seeds
- 1 tbsp pumpkin seeds
- 2 cups of spinach
- ¼ cup of raspberries
- ¼ cup of blueberries
- One whole banana halved
- Almond milk to the fill line

INSTRUCTIONS

1. In a sizeable nutribullet cup, combine all ingredients, save the almond milk for last.
2. Puree the ingredients till they reach the appropriate consistency after you've filled the cup with almond milk to the top of the waterline.

32. NUTRIBULLET GUACAMOLE

5 mins

Ingredients

- Ten servings
- Four large avocados
- Two green onions
- Two medium-sized tomatoes or four small tomatoes
- One bunch cilantro
- One large jalapeno or two small

- 1 tsp garlic powder or two pieces
- Two large lemons or four small
- 1 tsp black pepper as need
- 1 tbsp sour cream lite
- 1/4 red bell pepper

Instructions

1. Cut everything in half and place it in the nutribullet. If there are too many ingredients, do half at a time. Blend until smooth, then transfer to a bowl and set aside. Blend the remaining ingredients until smooth, then combine with the other half in the mixing bowl.
2. Stir, refrigerate for 30 minutes, then serve (if it's too difficult to combine, add a little water and trust me, it'll be delicious)

33. BLACK FOREST SMOOTHIE

Ingredients

- 1 cup of milk (plant milk if you like)
- One scoop of chocolate protein powder
- 1/2 cup of pitted frozen cherries
- 1/2 banana (optional)

Instructions

1. Place items in blender and blend until smooth.

34. EASY CHEESY BLENDER SCRAMBLED EGGS

prep time: 2 MINUTES

cook time: 3 MINUTES

total time: 5 MINUTES

Ingredients

- Three eggs
- ¼ Cup of milk
- 30g cheddar cheese
- Butter/oil (greasing the pan)

Instructions

2. In a blender, combine the eggs, milk, and cheese.
3. Immediately pour the egg mixture into a prepared non-stick pan.
4. Slowly stir the egg mixture around the pan with a wooden spoon till it reaches a soft consistency.
5. Serve your guests.

35. LOW-CALORIE NUTRIBULLET SMOOTHIE

INGREDIENTS

- 80g cantaloupe melon
- ½ ripe pear, chopped
- handful kale,
- ¼ roughly chopped cucumber,
- water or coconut water, to the line

INSTRUCTIONS

1. Fill the Nutribullet with all of the ingredients, including the water or coconut water, to the line.
2. Blitz all of the ingredients in a blender for about 1 minute or until you have a smooth smoothie consistency. Drink right away.

36. BLACK FOREST SMOOTHIE

Ingredients

- 1 cup of milk (plant milk if you like)
- One scoop of chocolate protein powder
- 1/2 cup of pitted frozen cherries
- 1/2 banana (optional)

Instructions

1. Blend the ingredients in a blender until smooth.
2. Smoothies for Breakfast That Are Good For You

3. Fresh or Frozen Fruit: You can make smoothies with a mix of frozen and fresh fruits—the frozen fruit aids in the thickening and creaming of the smoothie. Extra ripe bananas, peeled and split into smaller pieces, can be frozen and used in smoothies at any time. Because ice in a smoothie dilutes the flavor, use frozen fruit instead.
4. Vegetables: Vegetables are vitamin powerhouses, and incorporating them into your morning smoothies is a terrific way to start the day off right. Greens like spinach, kale, and other leafy greens work nicely in smoothies. You won't be able to tell if you put frozen cauliflower in a smoothie since you won't taste it. Try adding carrots to your morning smoothie if you have a high-powered blender for a healthy dose of sweetness.
5. Avocado smoothies: Have you ever tried one? Avocado adds healthy fats to a smoothie, combines smoothly, and has no flavor (as long as you don't use too much).

37. THE BEST BREAKFAST SMOOTHIE

Prep: 5 minutesCook: 0 minutes total: 5 minutes

INGREDIENTS

- One medium frozen banana
- 1 cup of frozen strawberries
- 2 tbsp rolled oatmeal
- ¼ cup of vanilla protein powder
- 1 tbsp all-natural creamy peanut butter
- 1 cup of plain unsweetened almond milk

INSTRUCTIONS

1. Place everything into a high-speed blender.
2. Blend on high, stopping to scrape the sides as needed until smooth.
3. Serve immediately!

NUTRITION FACTS

Serving Size: 1/2 Calories: 204 Sugar: 13 Sodium: 126 Fat: 6 Carbohydrates: 29 Fiber: 6 Protein: 12

38. 6 HEALTHY SUPERFOOD SMOOTHIES

Prep Time 5 mins

Total Time 5 mins

Ingredients

- Babe Ruth Strawberry Pineapple Banana Smoothie:
- 1 cup of Strawberries
- 1/2 cup of Pineapple
- 1 Banana
- 2 cups of Orange Juice
- 1/2 cup of Greek Yogurt
- 1 cup of spinach optional
- 1 Tbsp Chia
- Ice
- Sweet Cherry Almond Smoothie:
- 1 1/2 cups of Cherries frozen
- 1 cup of Almond Milk
- One scoop Protein Powder
- 1 BananaIce
- Optional: top with unsweetened coconut flakes + almond butter

Lovely Greens Smoothie:

- 1 cup of Pineapple
- 2 cups of Spinach
- 1/2 cup of Grapes
- 1 1/2 cup of Orange Juice
- 1 Banana
- Ice
- Chocolate Powerhouse Smoothie:
- 1 cup of Coconut Milk
- One scoop Chocolate Protein Powder
- 1/2 cup of Blueberries
- 1 cup of Spinach
- 1 Banana
- 1 Tbsp Almond Butter
- Ice

Instructions

1. Blend the ingredients in a blender until smooth and creamy. Depending on your preferred temperature, add ice.
2. Smoothies are best made with frozen bananas. First, peel the bananas, cut them in half, and freeze them overnight in a large Ziploc bag.
3. Increase the amount of spinach and kale in your salad to boost the nutritious value.

Nutrition Facts

6 Healthy Superfood Smoothies

Amount Per Serving

Calories 129 Calories from Fat 9

% Daily Value*

Fat 1g 2%

Cholesterol 1mg 0%

Sodium 17mg 1%

Potassium 522mg 15%

Carbohydrates 26g 9%

Fiber 2g 8%

Sugar 18g 20%

Protein 4g 8%

Vitamin A 970IU 19%

Vitamin C 97.7mg 118%

Calcium 61mg 6%

Iron 0.8mg 4%

39. HOW TO MAKE THE ULTIMATE HEALTHY BREAKFAST SMOOTHIE

Active Time 2 Mins

Total Time 3 Mins

Ingredients

- One medium banana (fresh or frozen) ½ cup of sliced strawberries, blueberries, or chopped mangos ¼ cup of 2% plain Greek yogurt 1 tbsp almond butter ½ cup of baby spinach ½ cup of unsweetened almond milk Optional: 1-2 basil leaves, 2-3 mint leaves, ½ tsp peeled, chopped ginger

Nutritional Information

Calories 300 Fat 11g Sat fat 1.5g Monofat 5g Polyfat 2g Protein 12.5g Sodium 135mg Carbohydrates 40g Fiber 7g Sugars 22g Added sugars 0g Calcium 20% DV Potassium 15%

40.5 HIGH PROTEIN FRUIT SMOOTHIE RECIPES FOR WEIGHT LOSS (5 INGREDIENTS OR LESS!)

Prep Time 2 mins

Cook Time 2 mins

Total Time 4 mins

Ingredients

- 1 cup of unsweetened almond milk
- 1/2 cup of frozen strawberries
- 1 tbsp peanut butter
- One scoop vanilla protein powder
- Fit + Slim Smoothie
- 1 cup of unsweetened almond milk
- 1 cup of frozen blueberries
- One scoop vanilla protein powder
- Chocolate + Coffee Smoothie
- 1 cup of unsweetened almond milk
- One frozen banana

- 1 tbsp freeze-dried coffee, or replace 1/4 cup of milk with 1/4 cup of chilled solid coffee
- 1/2 tbsp dark cocoa powder
- One scoop vanilla protein powder
- Green Machine Smoothie
- 1 cup of unsweetened almond milk
- frozen banana
- 1 cup of baby spinach, packed
- 1 tbsp peanut butter
- One scoop vanilla protein powder
- Vanilla Cup of cake Smoothie
- 1 cup of unsweetened almond milk
- 1/2 cup of frozen mango
- 1/2 cup of frozen pineapple
- One scoop vanilla protein powder

Instructions

1. Smoothie with Peanut Butter and Jelly
2. Begin by blending the unsweetened almond milk, frozen strawberries, peanut butter, and one scoop of vanilla protein powder in a kitchen blender.
3. Blend everything until it's completely smooth.
4. Smoothie to Keep You Fit and Slim
5. Begin by blending the unsweetened almond milk, frozen blueberries, and one scoop of vanilla protein powder in a kitchen blender.

Nutrition Facts

Amount Per Serving (1 smoothie)

Calories 156Calories from Fat 99

% Daily Value*

Fat 11g17%

Saturated Fat 2g10%

Cholesterol 2mg1%

Sodium 402mg17%

Potassium 214mg6%

Carbohydrates 10g3%

Fiber 3g12%

Sugar 5g6%

Protein 6g12%

Vitamin C 42mg51%

Calcium 312mg31%

Iron 1mg6%

41. OATMEAL SMOOTHIE

PREP:5 mins

TOTAL:5 mins

Ingredients

- 1/4 cup of old-fashioned oats or quick oats
- One banana chopped into chunks and frozen
- 1/2 cup of unsweetened almond milk
- 1 tbsp creamy peanut butter
- 1/2 tbsp pure maple syrup + additional as need
- 1/2 tsp pure vanilla extract
- 1/2 tsp ground cinnamon
- 1/8 tsp kosher salt, don't skip this, as it makes the oatmeal pop!
- Ice optional, add at the end if you want a thicker smoothie

Instructions

1. In the bottom of a blender, pulse the oats a few times until finely ground. Combine the banana, milk, peanut butter, maple syrup, vanilla, cinnamon, and salt in a large mixing bowl.
2. Blend until the mixture is smooth and creamy, scraping down the sides of the mixer as needed. If you want a sweeter smoothie, taste it and add more sweetener. Take pleasure at the moment.

Nutrition

SERVING: 1smoothie

CALORIES: 327kcal

CARBOHYDRATES: 54g

PROTEIN: 8g

FAT: 11g

SATURATED FAT: 2g

FIBER: 7g

SUGAR: 24g

42. GREEN PROTEIN POWER BREAKFAST SMOOTHIE

Prep Time: 5 minutes

Total Time: 5 minutes

INGREDIENTS

- 1 cup of (250 ml) unsweetened almond milk
- One ripe banana, frozen
- ½ cup of (125 ml) chopped mango, frozen
- 1-2 large handfuls of baby spinach
- ¼ cup of (60 ml) pumpkin seeds (pepita seeds)
- 2 tbsp (30 ml) hemp hearts (hulled hemp seeds)
- optional: ½ scoop (approx. 30ml) vanilla protein powder + ¼ cup of (60ml) water

INSTRUCTIONS

1. Layer the spinach, banana, mango, pumpkin seeds, and hemp hearts in a blender (or a large tumbler if using an immersion blender). Blend in the almond milk until the pumpkin seeds are entirely smooth. This recipe makes two large smoothies (500ml each).

43. PEANUT BUTTER BANANA SMOOTHIE

Prep: 5 mins

Total: 5 mins

Ingredients

- Two bananas, broken into chunks
- 2 cups of milk
- ½ cup of peanut butter
- 2 tbsp honey, or as need
- 2 cups of ice cubes

Directions

2. Place bananas, milk, peanut butter, honey, and ice cubes in a blender; blend until smooth, about 30 seconds.

44. PEANUT BUTTER BANANA SMOOTHIE

Prep: 5 mins

Total: 5 mins

Ingredients

- Two bananas, broken into chunks
- 2 cups of milk
- ½ cup of peanut butter
- 2 tbsp honey,
- 2 cups of ice cubes

Direction

3. Place bananas, milk, peanut butter, honey, and ice cubes in a blender; blend until smooth, about 30 seconds.

45. HOW TO MAKE A PERFECT GREEN SMOOTHIE

ACTIVE TIME: 5 minutes

TOTAL TIME: 5 minutes

Ingredients

- 2 cups of spinach
- 2 cups of water
- 1 cup of mango
- 1 cup of pineapple
- Two bananas, Use at least one frozen fruit to chill your smoothie. For example, we often use frozen mangos and bananas as our green smoothies.

Instructions

4. 2 cups leafy greens, tightly packed in a measuring cup, toss into blender
5. Blend in the water until all of the leaves bits are gone.
6. Blend in the mango, pineapple, and bananas until blended.
7. Pour into a mason jar
8. Gulp or sip like a rawk star!

46. HEALTHY BREAKFAST SMOOTHIE BERRY

Prep Time: 5 minutes

Blend: 3 minutes

Total Time: 8 minutes

Ingredients

- Two bananas
- 15 oz can every, undrained, or 2 cups of freshly sliced every

- 1 1/2 cups of fresh or frozen raspberries, blueberries, and blackberries (I use frozen berries for a thicker smoothie, but you can always add ice)
- 1/2 cup of old-fashioned rolled oats
- 1 cup of plain Greek yogurt or your favorite flavor
- large handful ice

Instructions

1. In a blender, combine fresh or frozen fruit. Pour in the liquid (milk, water, or low-sugar fruit juice). Combine old-fashioned oats, Greek yogurt, and a handful of ice cubes in a blender.
2. Blend until completely smooth. Add more ice (to thicken) or liquid (to thin) to achieve the correct consistency.

Nutrition

Calories: 192kcal | Carbohydrates: 39g | Protein: 8g | Fat: 1g | Cholesterol: 2mg | Sodium: 19mg | Potassium: 554mg | Fiber: 5g | Sugar: 22g | Vitamin A: 415IU | Vitamin C: 13.7mg | Calcium: 74mg | Iron: 1mg

47. WINTER BREAKFAST SMOOTHIE

Prep Time: 10 mins

Total Time: 10 mins

INGREDIENTS

- Three organic celery stalks, cleaned, peeled, and cut into medium pieces
- Two organic medium carrots, peeled and cut into medium pieces
- ½ organic large English cucumber, peeled, seeded, and cut into medium pieces
- One organic Granny Smith apple, peeled, cored, and cut into medium pieces
- 1 cup of fresh-squeezed blood orange juice (about six blood oranges)
- ¼ cup of freshly squeezed lime juice (or as need)

INSTRUCTIONS

1. Mix all the ingredients in a high-powered blender. Blend till smooth

48. SIMPLE GREEN SMOOTHIE

prep time: 5 MINUTES

cook time: 0 MINUTES

total time: 5 MINUTES

Ingredients

- 1 cup of almond milk (or more if needed to blend)
- 1 tbsp chia seeds
- 1 cup of spinach (not packed down)
- Two bananas, frozen
- 1 cup of mango (fresh or frozen)

Instructions

2. In a blender, combine all of the ingredients.
3. Begin blending on low, then increase to high for 20-30 seconds, or until smooth.
4. Serve by dividing the mixture between two glasses.

49. HEALTHY BREAKFAST SMOOTHIE – GLUTEN-FREE & VEGAN

Prep Time: 5 mins

Cook Time: 0 mins

Total Time: 5 minutes

INGREDIENTS

BASE SMOOTHIE INGREDIENTS:

- 4 Cups of Milk Alternative (1 cup per person)
- 1 Cup of Blueberries – Fresh or Frozen (1/4 cup of per person)
- 1 Cup of Strawberris or Black Cherries – Fresh or Frozen (1/4 cup of per person)
- 1 Banana – Fresh or Frozen (1/4 Banana per person)

- 1 Cup of Raw Cashews (1/4 Cup of per person) -OR- 1/2 Cup of Nut/Seed Butter (2 Tbsp per person)
- 4 Pitted Dates (1 Date per person)
- 1/4 Cup of Coconut Oil (1 Tbsp per person)
- 2–4 Drops Liquid Stevia – or as need (approx. 1 drop per person)
- 3 Cups of Ice (Approx. 3/4 Cups of Ice per person)

INSTRUCTIONS

1. Mix all Base Smoothie Ingredients + any Optional Ingredients – except ice – in a Vitamix.
2. Start on Variable Speed 1 and gradually increase to 10, then High. If necessary, use your Vitamix tamper to help push ingredients into the blades.
3. Blend until all of the components are thoroughly blended and the machine is working smoothly.
4. The consistency of the smoothie should be rich and creamy.
5. Add ice and blend on high until smooth, using your Vitamix tamper to help force items into the blades. The smoothie will start to thicken and set up.

50. GREEN BREAKFAST SMOOTHIE

PREP TIME: 5 MINS

COOK TIME: 0 MINS

TOTAL TIME: 5 MINS

INGREDIENTS

- 2 cups of spinach or kale leaves
- 2 cups of pineapple
- One medium banana
- 1/2 an apple, cored
- 2 tbsp hemp hearts, flax seeds,
- 2 cups of water

INSTRUCTIONS

1. Put all ingredients in a high-powered blender and blend for 1 minute.

51. BANANA OAT BREAKFAST SMOOTHIE

Prep Time: 5 mins

Total Time: 5 minutes

INGREDIENTS

- 1/3 cup of rolled oats
- 1/2 cup of yogurt (I used Silk Almondmilk yogurt)
- One banana
- 1 Tbsp flaxseed meal
- 1/2 tsp. cinnamon
- 1/2 cup of almond milk

INSTRUCTIONS

2. Add all ingredients to your blender and puree until smooth. Pour into two glasses, serve and enjoy!

NUTRITION FACTS:

SERVING SIZE: 1/2 OF RECIPE

CALORIES: 210

SUGAR: 13.3 G

SODIUM: 75.5 G

FAT: 7.5 G

SATURATED FAT: 0.6 G

CARBOHYDRATES: 32.5 G

FIBER: 4.8 G

PROTEIN: 5.6 G

52. HIGH FIBER SMOOTHIE

Prep Time5 mins

Total Time5 mins

Ingredients

- 1 cup of frozen blueberries
- One whole overripe banana fresh or frozen
- 1 cup of fresh spinach
- 2/3 cup of 1% milk
- 1/3 cup of plain Greek yogurt
- 1-2 tbsp. honey or maple syrup
- 1 tbsp. ground flax seed

Instructions

3. Place all ingredients in a blender, puree until smooth.

Nutrition

Calories: 213kcal | Carbohydrates: 38g | Protein: 9g | Fat: 5g | Saturated Fat: 1g | Cholesterol: 6mg | Sodium: 62mg | Potassium: 581mg | Fiber: 6g | Sugar: 26g | Vitamin A: 1640IU | Vitamin C: 17mg | Calcium: 177mg | Iron: 1mg

53. BANANA OATMEAL BREAKFAST SMOOTHIE

prep time: 2 MINUTES

cook time: 1 MINUTE

total time: 3 MINUTES

Ingredients

- 1/4 cup of oats (quick oats or old fashioned oats work great here)
- 3/4 cup of milk
- 1 tbsp peanut butter (or nut/seed butter of your choosing)
- One banana
- 4-5 ice cubes

Instructions

4. Add oatmeal, milk, peanut butter, banana, and ice cubes to the blender.
5. Blend about 1 minute until smooth. Enjoy immediately.

Nutrition Information:

YIELD: 1

Amount Per Serving: CALORIES: 387.03TOTAL FAT: 15.87gSATURATED FAT: 5.42gCHOLESTEROL: 4mgSODIUM: 83.78mgCARBOHYDRATES: 52.49gFIBER: 5.85gSUGAR: 25.27gPROTEIN: 13.24g

54. BREAKFAST ENERGY SMOOTHIE

Ingredients

- 2 cups of orange juice
- 1 cup of vanilla yogurt
- 1/2 tsp vanilla extract
- 2 cups of mixed fresh or frozen berries

Instructions

1. In a blender, combine all ingredients (liquid ingredients first).

Blend for 2 minutes on high, or until smooth. Blend for another 30 seconds after scraping down the sides.

Serve and enjoy!

55. CREAMSICLE BREAKFAST SMOOTHIE

Total: 5 mins

Ingredients

- 1 cup of cold pure coconut water, without added sugar or flavor (see Tip)
- 1 cup of nonfat vanilla Greek yogurt
- 1 cup of frozen
- 3 tbsp frozen orange juice concentrate
- 2 cups of ice

Nutrition Facts

184 calories; protein 12.7g; carbohydrates 32.9g; dietary fiber 2.7g; sugars 29g; fat 0.6g; saturated fat 0.3g; vitamin a iu 862.9IU; vitamin c 65.6mg; folate 54.3mcg; calcium 182.4mg; iron 0.6mg; magnesium 46.9mg; potassium 580.4mg; sodium 174.4mg; thiamin 0.1mg; added sugar 5g.

56. MY FAVORITE GREEN SMOOTHIE

PREP TIME 5 minutes

TOTAL TIME 5 minutes

Ingredients

- One medium banana (previously peeled, frozen, and quartered)
- 1/2 cup of mixed frozen berries
- 1 Tbsp flaxseed meal
- One heaping Tbsp natural, salted peanut butter
- 1/2 – 3/4 cup of unsweetened vanilla almond milk
- 2 cups of fresh spinach

Instructions

2. Blend all of the ingredients in a blender until smooth, adding more almond milk or frozen berries (or bananas) as needed to thin or thicken. Serve right now or freeze for later. It's best when it's still fresh...

57. PEVEY CRUMBLE SHAKE & 19 MORE VEGAN SMOOTHIES

PREP TIME 5 mins

TOTAL TIME 5 mins

INGREDIENTS

- Two ripe every – pitted, sliced and frozen
- ¼ cup of rolled oats
- One pitted Medjool date
- 1 tbsp chia seeds
- 1 tbsp almond butter
- big squeeze of fresh lemon juice
- ¾ tsp ground cinnamon
- ½ tsp vanilla extract
- One scoop vanilla protein powder, optional
- 1 cup of non-dairy milk
- ½ cup of filtered water

INSTRUCTIONS

3. Combine frozen peas, oats, date, chia seeds, almond butter, lemon juice, cinnamon, vanilla, protein powder (if using), non-dairy milk, and water in an upright blender. Blend on high until everything is well combined and foamy. It'll be pretty thick! Take pleasure at the moment.

58. BREAKFAST ENERGY SMOOTHIE

Ingredients

- 2 cups of orange juice
- 1 cup of vanilla yogurt
- 1/2 tsp vanilla extract
- 2 cups of mixed fresh or frozen berries

Instructions

1. Place all ingredients into a blender (liquid ingredients first).
2. Blend on high for 2 minutes or until smooth. Scrape down sides and blend for another 30 seconds.
3. Serve and enjoy!

59. BERRY BREAKFAST SMOOTHIE

INGREDIENTS

- 2 c unsweetened almond milk (or milk of choice)
- 2 c frozen berries (I used strawberries, blackberries, and raspberries)
- 1/2 frozen banana
- 1/4 c plain yogurt (I used greek yogurt for added protein)
- 2 tsp agave nectar
- 1 T chia seeds
- 1 T flaxseed

INSTRUCTIONS

Add everything to your blender or food processor and blend until smooth. ENJOY!!

60. HEALTHY OATMEAL SMOOTHIE

INGREDIENTS

- 1/2 cup of old-fashioned rolled oats
- 1 1/2 cups of frozen blueberries OR sliced frozen every
- 1 cup of vanilla yogurt
- 1/2 cup of almond milk
- 1 tbsp honey
- 1/4 tsp pure vanilla extract
- 1/4 tsp ground cinnamon, increase to 1/2 tsp if using every

INSTRUCTIONS

1. Blend the oats in a blender. Blend until a fine powder is formed. Frozen fruit, vanilla yogurt, milk, honey, vanilla, and cinnamon are combined in a bowl. Blend until the mixture is completely smooth. Serve right away.

61. POWER BREAKFAST SMOOTHIE

Total time: 10 minutes

Ingredients

- 1 cup of spinach
- 1 cup of Almond Breeze Original Almondmilk
- 1/2 banana
- 1/4 cup of blueberries
- 2 tbsp rolled oats
- 2 tbsp almond butter
- Two servings protein powder
- 1/4 cup of water, optional
- ice

Instructions

2. Combine the spinach, almond milk, banana, blueberries, rolled oats, almond butter, protein, water, and ice in a high-powered blender.
3. Blend until the mixture is smooth and creamy. Serve right away.

Nutrition

Calories: 299kcal, Carbohydrates: 21g, Protein: 31g, Fat: 13g, Saturated Fat: 1g, Cholesterol: 50mg, Sodium: 223mg, Potassium: 421mg, Fiber: 4g, Sugar: 8g, Vitamin A: 1487IU, Vitamin C: 9mg, Calcium: 318mg, Iron: 3mg

62. STRAWBERRY SUNRISE BREAKFAST SMOOTHIE

Prep Time 5 mins

Total Time 5 mins

INGREDIENTS

- 2 cups of strawberries
- One banana
- 1 cup of orange juice
- 1 cup of vanilla yogurt
- 2 tbsp flaxseed meal
- ½ tsp cinnamon
- Two handfuls ice

INSTRUCTIONS

1.
2. Place all ingredients in a high-speed blender and puree until smooth.
3. Serve in a large glass and enjoy.

NUTRITION

Calories: 287kcalCarbohydrates: 58.1gProtein: 8.1gFat: 4.2gSaturated Fat: 0.8gPolyunsaturated Fat: 3.6gCholesterol: 5mgSodium: 70mgFiber: 6.8gSugar: 41.8g

63. SUNRISE BREAKFAST SMOOTHIE

INGREDIENTS

- Sunrise Breakfast Smoothie
- 2 cups of coconut water
- 1 cups of Chobani Vanilla Greek Yogurt

- 1 cup of frozen strawberries
- 1 cup of frozen Pineapple
- One fresh orange peeled.

INSTRUCTIONS

1. In a blender, combine all ingredients and blend on high until thoroughly combined. To make the layers, combine 1/3 of the yogurt and coconut water with the strawberries, pineapple, and oranges individually. To produce a dawn impression, pour the orange first, then the strawberry, and finally the Pineapple

64. PEVERYES AND CREAM OATMEAL BREAKFAST SMOOTHIE

PREP TIME2 mins

COOK TIME0 mins

TOTAL TIME2 mins

INGREDIENTS

- 1 cup of frozen every slice
- 1 cup of Greek yogurt
- ¼ cup of oatmeal
- ¼ tsp vanilla extract
- 1 cup of almond milk

INSTRUCTIONS

2. Add all of the ingredients to a blender.
3. Blend until smooth.
4. Serve.

NUTRITION

Calories: 331kcal

65. GREEN BREAKFAST SMOOTHIE

Prep Time5 mins

Total Time 5 mins

Ingredients

- big handful of baby spinach
- One banana, frozen
- One scoop vanilla protein powder
- 1 tbsp almond butter
- 2 tbsp hemp hearts
- 1 cup of water, almond milk, oat milk, etc
- 1/4th tsp cinnamon

Instructions

1. Place all of the ingredients into the blender. Add a few ice cubes and blend until light and creamy. Pour and enjoy!

Nutrition

Serving: 1g | Calories: 437kcal | Carbohydrates: 38g | Protein: 30g | Fat: 21g | Saturated Fat: 2g | Cholesterol: 62mg | Sodium: 91mg | Potassium: 665mg | Fiber: 6g | Sugar: 17g | Vitamin A: 231IU | Vitamin C: 10mg | Calcium: 251mg | Iron: 5mg

66. BEET BANANA BREAKFAST SMOOTHIE

Prep Time 5 minutes

Total Time 5 minutes

Ingredients

- One ripe banana
- 1/2 pieces medium beetroot peeled and cut into 1-2."
- 1 1/2 tbsp chia seed
- 1/2 tsp vanilla
- 1 cup of skim milk (or almond milk if vegan)
- 1 tbsp honeyoptional

Instructions

2. Mix all ingredients in a blender and pulse until smooth. Adjust sweetener according to your taste.

Nutrition

Calories: 359kcal

67. CEREAL MILK BREAKFAST SMOOTHIE (3 WAYS!)

Prep: 5 minutes

Total: 5 minutes

Ingredients

For PB & Banana Breakfast Cereal Smoothie:

- 2 cups of LACTAID® 2% milk
- 1 cup of peanut butter puff style cereal lactose-free
- Two bananas sliced
- 1/2 cup of creamy peanut butter
- 1 cup of ice
- For Cinnamon & Honey Breakfast Cereal Smoothie:
- 2 cups of LACTAID® 2% milk
- 1 cup of Cinnamon Chex or comparable lactose-free cereal

Instructions

3. Mix all ingredients in a high-powered blender and blend until smooth.
4. Enjoy!

68. CINNAMON ROLL BREAKFAST SMOOTHIE

PREP TIME: 5 MINUTES

TOTAL TIME: 5 MINUTES

INGREDIENTS

- 1/2 cup of rolled oats
- 3/4 cup of plain greek yogurt
- 1 Tbsp brown sugar/coconut sugar
- 1 cup of almond milk

- 1 tsp cinnamon
- 1/2 tsp vanilla
- One frozen banana

INSTRUCTIONS

1. Place all the ingredients into your blender.
2. Blend until smooth.
3. Serve and enjoy.

NUTRITION

CALORIES: 220KCAL | CARBOHYDRATES: 37G | PROTEIN: 11G | FAT: 3G | CHOLESTEROL: 3MG | SODIUM: 193MG | POTASSIUM: 390MG | FIBER: 4G | SUGAR: 15G | VITAMIN A: 40IU | VITAMIN C: 5.1MG | CALCIUM: 256MG | IRON: 1.1MG

69. CLEAN EATING BREAKFAST SMOOTHIE

Ingredients

- 2 Ripe Bananas
- 5 Tbsp Chia Seeds
- 2/3 Cup of Organic Oats
- 1 tsp honey
- 1 tsp vanilla extract
- One handful Almonds
- 2 cups of Almond milk

Instructions

Combine all ingredients in a blender and blend until smooth.

Allow for a couple of minutes in the blender / or glass before serving to allow the smoothie to thicken up beautifully.

Note

If you want your smoothies colder, use frozen bananas or a few ice cubes when making them.

This recipe serves TWO LARGE SERVINGS, so double it if necessary. If you're making it for small children, this will help 3 to 4 children.

70. FROZEN FRUIT SMOOTHIES

Ingredients

- One ripe banana
- One glass of frozen fruit
- Two heaped tbsp natural yogurt
- One small handful of oats
- One small handful of mixed nuts
- One glass of organic soya milk, skimmed milk, or apple juice
- honey, as need, optional

Method

1. Peel and slice your banana, then blend it with the frozen fruit and yogurt in a blender. Blend it till smooth, then add the grains and nuts. Whiz in the soy milk, skimmed milk, or apple juice until completely smooth. If it's a little too thick, add a splash of milk or juice and whiz it around again. Give it a nice stir before tasting it. You shouldn't need to sweeten a frozen fruit smoothie very often, but if you think it needs a little extra sweetness, add a little honey as required - you won't need much...

71. MANGO SMOOTHIE

Prep Time 5 minutes

Total Time 5 minutes

Ingredients

- 1 cup of nonfat milk
- 1 cup of greek yogurt (plain, vanilla, or honey will work)
- 1 ½ cups of ice cubes
- One banana (if frozen, leave out some of the ice)
- One mango (about 1 cup of chopped)
- ⅛ cup of unsweetened coconut
- 1 tsp vanilla extract
- 1 tbsp honey

- chia seeds (optional)

Instructions

2. In a blender, combine all ingredients and process until smooth, about 3 minutes.
3. If preferred, top with chia seeds, more coconut, and diced mango.

Nutrition

Calories: 288kcal | Carbohydrates: 49g | Protein: 16g | Fat: 5g | Saturated Fat: 3g | Cholesterol: 7mg | Sodium: 92mg | Potassium: 746mg | Fiber: 4g | Sugar: 40g | Vitamin A: 1408IU | Vitamin C: 43mg | Calcium: 271mg | Iron: 1mg

72. MAKE-AHEAD SMOOTHIES

prep time: 20 MINUTES

total time: 20 MINUTES

Ingredients

- 1 cup of almond milk
- One scoop protein powder
- 1 Tbsp chia seeds
- 1 cup of frozen berries
- One handful spinach

Instructions

1. In a blender, combine all of the ingredients. I usually make two or three smoothies at a time. If I create 5, the blender won't be able to handle it.
2. Fill the 2-cup mason jars halfway with the smoothie, leaving some room at the top. Otherwise, they will expand, potentially shattering the glass.
3. Keep frozen until you're ready for a quick breakfast on the run.

73. BEST GREEN JUICE

Ingredients

- 5 or 6 kale leaves

- handful spinach leaves (with stems)
- 1/2 lemon, peeled
- One Honeycrisp apple, core removed
- 1/2 field cucumber (peel the skin, if tough)
- Two ribs celery
- One small carrot
- 1" piece ginger, peeled

Instructions

1. In your juicer, process all of the ingredients according to the manufacturer's instructions. Drink right away or chill for an hour or two.

Nutrition

Calories: 36kcal

74. METABOLISM, BALANCED MEAL, GREAT FOR HAIR, SKIN, AND NAILS}

Prep Time: 5 minutes

Total Time: 5 minutes

Ingredients

- 6 ounces of freshly brewed coffee
- 8 ounces of milk or coconut milk
- 1-2 raw egg yolks
- 2 tbsp collagen
- 1 tbsp of maple syrup or your preferred sweetener as need
- 1-3 tsp coconut oil

Instructions

2. In a large glass, combine all of the ingredients.
3. To combine everything smoothly, use a hand blender. (This is the one I use, and it's fantastic!)
4. If necessary, you can also use a regular blender to combine everything. Blend until completely smooth.
5. Note: If using hot coffee, blend all of the other ingredients first before adding the coffee. Otherwise, your egg yolks may become overcooked, which isn't ideal... awful.

Nutrition Facts

Calories 465Calories from Fat 270

% Daily Value*

Fat 30g46%

Saturated Fat 19g119%

Polyunsaturated Fat 2g

Monounsaturated Fat 7g

Cholesterol 392mg131%

Sodium 147mg6%

Potassium 464mg13%

75.APPLE COBBLER SMOOTHIE
Ingredients

- 1 cups of spinach
- 1/4 cup of zucchini, fresh
- 1/2Banana
- 1/2 cup ofRed Apple
- One tbsp walnuts, raw, unsalted
- 1 1/2 cup of almond milk, unsweetened
- One tbsp oats, rolled, gluten-free
- 1/4 tspCinnamon, ground

Directions

1 Add ingredients in the order listed and blend until smooth.

2 Enjoy!

Nutritional information

Recipe: Apple Cobbler Smoothie

Serving in this recipe: 1

Calories: 216.7

Total Fat: 8.4 g   12.9%

Saturated Fat: 0.8 g   4.2%

Cholesterol: 0 mg   0%

Sodium: 286.9 mg   12%

Total Carbs: 33.8 g   11.3%

76. APPLE A DAY
Ingredients

- 1 cups of spinach
- 1/2 Avocado
- 1 Green Apple
- 1/4 cup of walnuts, raw, unsalted
- 1 1/2 cup of almond milk, unsweetened
- 1/2 tsp Cinnamon, ground

Directions

1. Add ingredients in the order listed and blend until smooth
2. Enjoy!

Nutritional information

Recipe: Apple a Day

Serving in this recipe: 1

Calories: 472.2

Total Fat: 34 g   52.3%

77. APPLE PIE SMOOTHIE

PREP TIME 5 minutes

COOK TIME 5 minutes

TOTAL TIME 10 minutes

INGREDIENTS

- 2 cups of your favorite apples
- ½ cup of low-fat vanilla yogurt
- 1 tsp. of cinnamon
- A dash of nutmeg
- Vanilla soy milk to the max line

INSTRUCTIONS

1. Fill the Nutribulletcup, add water to the max line (if needed) and blend.

Nutrition Information:

Amount Per Serving: CALORIES: 208TOTAL FAT: 1.6gSATURATED FAT: 1.3gCHOLESTEROL: 7mgSODIUM: 88mgCARBOHYDRATES: 40.7gFIBER: 6.5gSUGAR: 31.4gPROTEIN: 7.1g

78. APPLE PEAR GINGER SMOOTHIE

Prep Time10 mins

Total Time10 mins

Ingredients

- ½ cup of Rolled Oats
- 3 Applesdiced – red, peeled, cored
- 3 Pears – sweetdiced, peeled, cored
- One thumbfinely grated-size fresh ginger,
- 1½ cup of Apple Juice

Instructions

2. Pulse the oats in a food processor (or a blender) until they resemble powder. Blend in the rest of the ingredients until smooth (see note 6).
3. Best served right away!

79. SANTA BARBARA TROPICAL GINGER SMOOTHIE RECIPE

TOTAL TIME 5 minutes

Ingredients

- 1 cup of Pineapple
- 1 cup of frozen mango pieces
- One ripe fresh or frozen ripe banana
- 1 cup of coconut milk
- Two tangerines peeled
- 1-inch fresh ginger peeled and grated
- 1 tbsp honey

Instructions

1. Mix everything except cinnamon in a blender and process until smooth. Garnish with cinnamon and serve.

80. TROPICAL GINGER SMOOTHIE

PREP TIME: 10 MINUTES

Ingredients

- One ripe frozen banana
- 1½ cups of mango
- ½ cup of fresh-squeezed orange juice
- ¼ cup of unsweetened almond milk
- 1 tsp freshly grated Ginger
- 1 tsp fresh lime juice
- 1 tbsp white chia seeds Yes, you can use black, but you will end up with black dots in your smoothie. No biggie, but not

81. TROPICAL GREEN SMOOTHIE

Prep Time 5 mins

Total Time 5 mins

INGREDIENTS

- One banana
- 1 cup of mango fresh or frozen, cubed
- 1 cup of pineapple, fresh or frozen, cubed
- Two inch-piece ginger thinly sliced
- 2 tbsp lemon juice
- 4 cups of dark leafy greens such as kale, spinach, cilantro, parsley
- 2 tbsp flaxseed meal
- 1 cup of water
- ice as need

INSTRUCTIONS

2. In a high-powered blender, purée all of the ingredients until smooth. To thicken, add ice cubes until you reach the desired consistency. To serve, divide the mixture among four glasses...

NUTRITION

Serving: 1glassCalories: 99kcalCarbohydrates: 21gProtein: 2gFat: 2gSaturated Fat: 1gSodium: 29mgPotassium: 416mgFiber: 4gSugar: 14gVitamin A: 3302IUVitamin C: 49mgCalcium: 49mgIron: 1mg

82. TROPICAL MANGO PINEAPPLE SMOOTHIE

Prep Time5 mins

Total Time5 mins

Ingredients

- Two cups of Pineapple 450g. preferably ripe.
- One cup of mango 160g. preferably frozen
- One ripe banana
- 1/2 cup of orange juice 80ml.
- One cup of water 250ml.
- a small handful of fresh mint

Instructions

3. In a blender, combine all of the ingredients and blend until smooth. To achieve the correct consistency, add more water or orange juice.

Depending on the blender, varying amounts of liquid may be required.

83. TROPICAL TUMERIC GINGER SMOOTHIE

PREP TIME 5 mins

1/2 cup of pineapple frozen

1/2 cup of guava frozen

2 inches turmeric root skin removed

1/2 inch ginger root skin removed

1/4 cup of banana frozen

1 cup of fresh orange juice

INSTRUCTIONS

4. Place all ingredients in the blender and blend until smooth. Pour into a glass and enjoy.

84. TROPICAL CARROT JUICE

Prep: 5 minutes

Total: 5 minutes

Ingredients

- 1 cup of chopped carrots
- One large mango peeled and chopped
- 1 cup of chopped pineapple fresh or canned in juice
- 1 tsp fresh grated ginger
- 1/4 cup of water

Instructions

5. Blend: In a blender, combine all ingredients and blitz until smooth.
6. To make this carrot juice smooth and velvety, you have two options.
7. Pour the mixture through a nut milk bag to filter away the fibers for a juice-like consistency.

8. Add a splash of water or pineapple juice to the blender and pulse for a thicker consistency.
9. If your fruit wasn't cold, to begin with, chill the juice until it's cooled before serving, or serve over ice.

Nutrition Information

Serving: 1cup of Calories: 84kcal (4%) Carbohydrates: 21g (7%) Protein: 1.2g (2%) Fat: 0.4g (1%) Saturated Fat: 0.1g (1%) Cholesterol: 0mg Sodium: 20mg (1%) Potassium: 280mg (8%) Fiber: 2.7g (11%) Sugar: 16.9g (19%) Calcium: 20mg (2%) Iron: 0.4mg (2%

85. THE BEST DETOX GREEN SMOOTHIE RECIPE

PREP TIME 10 mins

TOTAL TIME 10 mins

INGREDIENTS

- 1 cup of unsweetened almond milk
- 1 banana, frozen
- ½ cup of pineapple, frozen
- 1 tsp fresh ginger, grated
- 1 handful chopped kale
- ⅛ tsp cinnamon

INSTRUCTIONS

1. Put all the ingredients in a blender and mix well.

NUTRITION

Calories: 198kcalCarbohydrates: 45gProtein: 6gFat: 4gSaturated Fat: 1gSodium: 353mgPotassium: 841mgFiber: 5gSugar: 23gVitamin A: 6769IUVitamin C: 130mgCalcium: 411mgIron: 2mg

86. GINGER MATCHA SMOOTHIE BOWL

PREP TIME 3 mins

COOK TIME 2 mins

TOTAL TIME 5 mins

INGREDIENTS

- 1 cup of Greek Yogurt
- 1/2 cup of diced mango
- 1/2 cup of pineapple chunks
- 1/2 tsp matcha powder
- 1/2-1 tbs fresh grated ginger

INSTRUCTIONS

2. Place all ingredients in a blender and process at medium to high speed until smooth.
3. Transfer to a bowl and add your favorite toppings

87. SMOOTHIES 101: A PEDIATRICIAN'S PRESCRIPTION

Ingredients

- Mixed Berry and Beet Smoothie
- 1 cup of mixed frozen berries or blueberries
- 2 tsp chia seeds
- 2 tsp ground flax seeds
- 1/4 tsp ground cinnamon
- 1/2 tbsp walnuts
- 1/3 cup of diced beet, either raw, canned, or roasted
- Handful fresh or 1-2 tbsp frozen spinach
- 1/4 cup of plain low-fat yogurt
- One frozen banana

Directions

1. Place all of the ingredients in a blender and blend for one full minute.
2. Pour into a glass and enjoy.

Nutrition Information (per serving)

Calories: 372

Fat: 14 g

Cholesterol: 0

Trans fat: 0

Saturated fat: 1.5 g

Sodium: 78 mg

88. GOLDEN MILK TROPICAL TURMERIC SMOOTHIE

Prep Time: 15 mins

Total Time: 15 mins

INGREDIENTS

- 2 1/2 cup of fresh pineapple chunks, 8 ounces
- 3 cups of frozen mango chunks, 10 ounces
- One ripe banana, peeled
- 1 Tbsp minced fresh ginger
- 1/2 Tsp ground turmeric
- 1/2 Tsp ground cinnamon
- Pinch of black pepper
- 1 cup of coconut milk from the can
- 1-2 cups of water

INSTRUCTIONS

1. In a blender, combine all of the ingredients in the order stated.
2. Secure the cover and mix on low for a few minutes before increasing to high.
3. Blend until entirely smooth, scraping down the sides of the bowl as needed to keep the mixture moving.
4. Within one day, serve.

89. THE CHEEKY MONKEY SMOOTHIE

Prep Time: 5 minutes

Total Time: 5 minutes

Ingredients

- Juice of ½ Lime

- One medium Banana
- 1 tsp fresh ginger, peeled and rough chopped
- Three medium Kale leaves (without stem), torn into pieces
- ½ cup of fresh pineapple, rough chopped
- 1 cup of 'Super Greens' (these can be purchased in the salad area already prepared or mixed at home by combining baby red chard, baby tatsoi, baby spinach, baby green Swiss chard, and baby arugula)
- ½ cup of filtered water

Instructions

1. Place water in a blender followed by the other ingredients.
2. Blend until smooth.

Nutrition

Calories: 238kcal | Carbohydrates: 54g | Protein: 9g | Fat: 2g | Saturated Fat: 0g | Cholesterol: 0mg | Sodium: 97mg | Potassium: 1519mg | Fiber: 4g | Sugar: 22g | Vitamin A: 19970IU | Vitamin C: 263.3mg | Calcium: 297mg | Iron: 3.9mg

90. EASY DELICIOUS TROPICAL GREEN SMOOTHIE

Prep Time 5 minutes

Ingredients

- One small frozen banana
- 1/2 cup of frozen pineapple heaping
- 1 cup of liquid
- 1/4 cup of cucumber
- 1 cup of spinach packed
- 1 tbsp flaxseed
- 2 tbsp unflavoured collagen or protein powder
- 1/2 tsp cinnamon
- 1/4 tsp fresh ginger
- 1/4 tsp turmeric powder
- 3-6 ice cubes

Instructions

1. To begin, pour 3/4 cup of liquid and all of the spinach into a Vitamix blender. Blend on high to break down all of the leafy bits.

2. Blend the remaining ingredients in a Vitamix on low speed till smooth, then increase to high.
3. Blend on high for another 50-60 seconds, or until the mixture is smooth. If you prefer a slightly thinner smoothie, add the remaining 1/4 cup of liquid at this step!

91. TROPICAL GREEN FLAXSEED SMOOTHIE

PREP TIME: 5 MINUTES

TOTAL TIME: 5 MINUTES

INGREDIENTS

- 3/4 cup of frozen Pineapple
- 1 cup of fresh baby spinach, packed
- 1/2 tbsp lime juice
- 3/4 tsp ground ginger
- 1/2 cup of plant-based milk
- 1/2 cup of lite coconut milk
- 2 tbsp Manitoba Milling Company Smooth Whole-Milled Flaxseed, 1 tbsp for low FODMAP version
- pinch salt

INSTRUCTIONS

1. Mix all ingredients in a blender and blend until smooth.

NUTRITION

Serving: 1serving | Calories: 251kcal | Carbohydrates: 27g | Protein: 5g | Fat: 14g | Saturated Fat: 7g | Sodium: 276mg | Potassium: 416mg | Fiber: 7g | Sugar: 13g | Vitamin A: 2885IU | Vitamin C: 70mg | Calcium: 231mg | Iron: 2mg

92. SUNSHINE SMOOTHIE BOWL

Prep Time: 5 minutes

Total Time: 5 minutes

Ingredients

- 2/3 cup of plain whole-milk Greek yogurt (I used Fage 5%)
- 1/2 cup of frozen mango chunks
- 1/2 small frozen banana
- 1/2 cup of 100% orange juice
- 1 tsp fresh ginger, grated
- 1/8 tsp ground turmeric
- 1/8 tsp cinnamon
- optional toppings: orange slice, toasted coconut flakes, granola, sliced banana, extra spices, hemp hearts

Instructions

2. Add all ingredients to a blender and mix until smooth and creamy. Pour into a bowl and add preferred toppings.

93. SWEET GINGER BASIL SMOOTHIE

PREP TIME 5 mins

TOTAL TIME 5 mins

INGREDIENTS

- 1/4 cup of fresh basil leaves
- 1/2 cup of Pineapple
- 1 tbsp ginger root
- 1/2 cup of mango
- One banana or 1/4 cup of banana powder
- 1 tbsp chia seeds
- 3 cups of water
- 1 cup of ice
- One scoop protein powder optional

INSTRUCTIONS

3. Add all ingredients to a high-speed blender.
4. Blend on low, and increase speed until all fruit/ice chunks are blended, and the smoothie is a creamy consistency.
5. Pour into your favorite glass, sit back, and enjoy!

94. VANILLA MANGO SPINACH SMOOTHIE

PREP TIME: 5 MINUTES

TOTAL TIME: 5 MINUTES

INGREDIENTS

- 1 cup of frozen mango chunks
- 1 cup of packed fresh baby spinach leaves
- ¾ cup of unsweetened almond milk
- 1 to 2 tsp freshly grated
- Ginger
- One scoop vanilla protein powder*
- ½ to 1 tbsp honey or pure maple syrup**
- 1 tbsp ground flaxseed
- 1 tsp vanilla extract
- few tbsp glasses of water, if needed

INSTRUCTIONS

1. In a blender, mix all of the ingredients except the water. Blend the mixture until it is smooth. If necessary, add a splash of water to thin down the smoothie or start it going in the blender. Serve right away.

NUTRITION INFORMATION:

Amount Per Serving: Calories: 372Total Fat: 7gSaturated Fat: 1gTrans Fat: 0gUnsaturated Fat: 6gCholesterol: 5mgSodium: 184mgCarbohydrates: 47gFiber: 11gSugar: 33gProtein: 34g

95. SUNSHINE TROPICAL SMOOTHIE WITH TURMERIC

Prep Time: 3 minutes

Total Time: 3 minutes

Ingredients

- 2 cups of frozen mango
- 2 cups of frozen Pineapple
- 2 tbsp lime juice from 2-4 limes
- 2 tsp coconut butter
- 2 tbsp fresh turmeric peeled and chopped
- 2 1/4 cups of cold coconut water the new stuff
- tiny pinch cinnamon for garnish

Instructions

2. Mix the frozen fruit, lime juice, coconut butter, turmeric, and coconut water in a blender. Blend on high until completely smooth. Serve immediately with a pinch of cinnamon.

96. VEGAN TROPICAL BUTTERNUT SQUASH SMOOTHIE

total time: 5 MINUTES

Ingredients

¼ cup of mango (frozen)

¼ cup of pineapple chunks (frozen)

¼ cup of butternut squash (frozen)

8 oz. coconut water

1-inch ginger root

Six basil or mint leaves

Instructions

3. Use fresh food that has been frozen overnight in a ziplock bag.
4. To make a smoothie, combine all of the ingredients in a blender and blend until smooth. If the smoothie is too thick, add a bit of coconut water to thin it down.
5. Enjoy it with a garnish of mint or basil leaves or even berries.

97. IMMUNE BOOSTER SWEET GREEN SMOOTHIE

Prep Time5 minutes

Total Time 5 minutes

Ingredients

- 1 cup of roughly chopped spinach and kale, packed tightly
- 1 1/2 cups of Almond Breeze Unsweetened Almondmilk
- 1 1/2 cups of a frozen mix of mango, pineapple, and kiwi chunks
- 1/2 tsp freshly grated Ginger
- 1/2 lemon, juiced

Instructions

1. Blend the spinach and kale with the Almond Breeze in a blender until smooth.
2. Blend in the frozen fruit, ginger, and lemon until entirely smooth. Add more almond milk if the smoothie is too thick. 1 tbsp at a time is a good starting point.

Nutrition

Serving: 2g | Calories: 112kcal | Carbohydrates: 22g | Protein: 3g | Fat: 3g | Saturated Fat: 1g | Sodium: 257mg | Potassium: 329mg | Fiber: 4g | Sugar: 18g | Vitamin A: 2746IU | Vitamin C: 64mg | Calcium: 260mg | Iron: 1mg

98. GREEN APPLE LEMON CUCUMBER GINGER SMOOTHIE

PREP TIME: 10 mins

TOTAL TIME: 10 mins

INGREDIENTS

- 3/4 cup of coconut water
- Two green apples, cored and quartered
- 1/4 English cucumber, chopped
- 1/2 bunch flat-leaf parsley, leaves only, chopped
- One slice piece ginger, 1 inch thick
- One medium lemon, peeled and seeded
- 1 cup of ice cubes

INSTRUCTIONS

1. In a high-powered blender, combine all of the ingredients, starting with the liquids, and blend until smooth. If you don't want it pulpy, strain it through a mesh sieve. Then, pour into two ice-filled glasses.
2. Pour into two ice-filled glasses...

99. GREEN SMOOTHIE RECIPE - MAKE IT YOUR OWN!

INGREDIENTS

One handful of spinach (about 1 ½ cups of)

One handful of kale (about 1 ½ cups of)

1 Granny Smith apple, cored and diced

1 cup of cold water,

1 cup of tropical frozen fruit mix (strawberries, pineapple, mango)

½ cup of ice

INSTRUCTIONS

1. In a blender, combine spinach, kale, apple, and water. Blend until completely smooth. Blend in the frozen tropical fruit until smooth. If required, add ice and more water (or milk) until the required consistency is achieved.
2. Refrigerate any leftovers. Drink right away or within three days for the most excellent flavor.

100. TROPICAL FRUIT SMOOTHIE WITH COCONUT FLOUR

Total: 5 mins

Ingredient

- ½ cup of pineapple (frozen)
- One mango (peeled, pitted, and diced)
- One banana (medium)

- ¼ cup of coconut milk (canned)
- 1 tsp coconut flour
- 1 cup of water

Instructions

1. In a blender, mix all of the ingredients and blend until very smooth. For a thinner smoothie, add more water.

101. CARROT APPLE GINGER SMOOTHIE

Prep Time 5 minutes

Total Time 5 minutes

Ingredients

- One c. baby carrots
- 1/2 - 1 " ginger about 1 tbsp freshly grated ginger
- One apple cored and chopped
- One banana peeled
- juice from half a lemon
- 1/2 c. ice
- 1/2 c. water

Instructions

2. In a blender, combine the water, lemon juice, banana, carrots, apple, and ginger. For around 30 seconds, blend.
3. To thicken, add 1/2 c. to 1 c. ice as needed. Blend for another 30-60 seconds.

102. WATCH HOW TO MAKE COFFEE SMOOTHIE

Prep Time 5 mins

Total Time 5 mins

Ingredients

- 1 cup of strong brewed coffee
- One banana
- 1/4- a cup of rolled oats
- 1 tbsp cocoa powder
- 1 tbsp flaxseeds meal
- 1/8 tsp ground cinnamon
- 1 cup of soy milk or almond milk
- 1 tsp honey

Instructions

1. Pour coffee into an ice cube tray and freeze overnight.
2. Mix all the ingredients in a blender, including the coffee ice cubes, and blend until smooth.
3. Taste for sweetness and adjust accordingly.
4. Serve.

Nutrition Facts

Coffee Smoothie

Amount Per Serving

Calories 144Calories from Fat 36

% Daily Value*

Fat 4g6%

Sodium 167mg7%

Potassium 372mg11%

Carbohydrates 26g9%

Fiber 4g16%

Sugar 10g11%

Protein 3g6%

Vitamin A 40IU1%

Vitamin C 5.1mg6%

Calcium 164mg 16%

Iron 1.1mg 6%

103. PERCENT DAILY VALUES ARE BASED ON A 2000 CALORIE DIET.

PREP TIME 5 mins

TOTAL TIME 5 mins

INGREDIENTS

- Coffee: I like to use cold brew coffee for the best flavor, but you can use instant if that's what you have.
- Oats: Rolled oats add fiber and antioxidants and will help to keep you feeling full.
- Banana: Use an overripe banana which will be naturally sweeter and contains more antioxidants.
- Milk: You can use any milk you like in this recipe, dairy or plant-based.
- Protein powder: I like to use a vanilla-flavored protein powder to give me the energy I need to face the day!
- Cocoa powder and cinnamon: For flavor

INSTRUCTIONS

1. Put all the ingredients in a high-speed blender and blend under desired consistency. Enjoy immediately

NUTRITION

Serving: 1cup
of, Calories: 377kcal, Carbohydrates: 54g, Protein: 27g, Fat: 7g, Saturated Fat: 3g, Cholesterol: 73mg, Sodium: 132mg, Potassium: 817mg, Fiber: 5g, Sugar: 22g, Vitamin A: 275IU, Vitamin C: 10.2mg, Calcium: 302mg, Iron: 1.5mg

104. COFFEE SMOOTHIE | HEALTHY BLENDED COFFEE!

PREP TIME 5 minutes

TOTAL TIME 5 minutes

INGREDIENTS

- 1/2 cup of brewed coffee (not hot)
- 3 to 4 Medjool dates, pitted (soak in hot water for 15 minutes if they are not soft)*
- 1 tbsp hemp hearts
- 1 tbsp nut butter
- 1 cup of ice cubes,

INSTRUCTIONS

2. Mix the coffee, three dates, hemp hearts, and nut butter in a high-powered blender. Blend until the mixture is completely smooth. Taste the mix, and if it needs to be sweeter, add more date.

NUTRITION

Calories: 386kcal | Carbohydrates: 58g | Protein: 10g | Fat: 16g | Saturated Fat: 1g | Sodium: 16mg | Potassium: 679mg | Fiber: 7g | Sugar: 49g | Vitamin A: 185IU | Calcium: 132mg | Iron: 3mg

105. CREAMY COFFEE & BANANA SMOOTHIE

PREP TIME 8 mins

TOTAL TIME 8 mins

INGREDIENTS

- One frozen banana
- Two Medjool dates or 1 1/2 tbsp honey
- 1 1/2 tbsp almond or hazelnut butter
- 1 cup of unsweetened almond milk
- 3/4 cup of strong brewed coffee
- 1 1/2 cup of frozen cauliflower florets
- pinch of salt

INSTRUCTIONS

3. In a blender, mix all of the ingredients and blend until smooth. If the smoothie is too thick, add additional almond milk to thin it up.

NUTRITION

Calories: 166kcal

Carbohydrates: 18g

Protein: 5g

Fat: 9g

Sodium: 188mg

Sugar: 8g

106. COFFEE PROTEIN SMOOTHIE

Prep: 5

Cook: 5

Total: 10minutes

Ingredients

- 2/3 cup of coffee, cold
- 6–8 ice cubes
- One frozen banana
- 1 tbsp cocoa powder
- 1 tbsp almond butter
- 1/4 cup of protein powder
- 2 tbsp chia seeds

Instructions

4. Combine all smoothie ingredients in a high-powered blender.
5. Allow 15-20 seconds for the blender to run until perfectly smooth.
6. Add additional coffee or almond milk if it's too thick.
7. Serve

Nutrition Facts

Serving Size 1 serving

Serves 1

Amount Per Serving

Calories 385

% Daily Value*

Total Fat 18.1g   23%

Cholesterol 0.9mg   0%

Sodium 38.6mg   2%

107. HEALTHY PROTEIN COFFEE SMOOTHIE

PREP TIME 5 mins

TOTAL TIME 5 mins

INGREDIENTS

- 3/4 cup of dairy-free milk,
- 1 cup of fresh spinach
- 2 tbsp cocoa powder
- Three dates
- 1 tbsp pea protein
- 2 tsp chia seeds
- ½ tsp finely ground espresso
- ¼ tsp vanilla bean powder, or you can use vanilla extract
- ¼ tsp cinnamon
- ¼ tsp sea salt
- 12 ice cubes

INSTRUCTIONS

1. Add everything into a blender.
2. Blend until smooth and creamy.

NUTRITION

Calories: 238kcal

Carbohydrates: 28g

Protein: 21g

Fat: 8g

Saturated Fat: 1g

108. COFFEE SMOOTHIE WITH BANANA AND OATS

Prep Time: 5 minutes

Total Time: 5 minutes

Ingredients

- 1 cup of brewed coffee
- 1 cup of milk
- ⅓ cup of quick oats
- One frozen banana
- 1 tbsp honey (optional)
- ⅓ cup of Greek yogurt

Instructions

1. Place all of the ingredients into a blender.
2. Blend until smooth.

Nutrition

Calories: 458kcal | Carbohydrates: 77g | Protein: 20g | Fat: 10g | Saturated Fat: 5g | Cholesterol: 28mg | Sodium: 136mg | Potassium: 1050mg | Fiber: 6g | Sugar: 47g | Vitamin A: 471IU | Vitamin C: 10mg | Calcium: 362mg | Iron: 2mg

109. LOADED COFFEE SMOOTHIE

Ingredients

- One medium banana previously sliced and frozen
- 1/2 cup of strong brewed coffee, chilled 120 mL
- 1/2 cup of milk (any variety) 120 mL
- 1/4 cup of rolled oats 25 g
- Optional: a spoonful of nut butter

Instructions

1. Mix all ingredients in a blender until smooth, adding more milk as necessary to every consistency to your liking. Optionally top with a sprinkle of chocolate and serve immediately.

Nutrition

Serving: 1smoothie | Calories: 257cal | Carbohydrates: 46g | Protein: 7g | Fat: 5g | Saturated Fat: 2g | Cholesterol: 12mg | Sodium: 57mg | Potassium: 714mg | Fiber: 5g | Sugar: 20g | Vitamin A: 275IU | Vitamin C: 10.2mg | Calcium: 148mg | Iron: 1.2mg

110. COFFEE PROTEIN SHAKE RECIPE

Prep: 5 minutes

Cook: 0 minutes

Total: 5 minutes

INGREDIENTS

One large frozen banana

2 tbsp all-natural creamy peanut butter

1/4 cup of powder (both vanilla and chocolate are delicious)

¼ cup of cold brew concentrate*

1/2 cup of unsweetened almond milk

INSTRUCTIONS

2. Place all ingredients into a high-speed blender.
3. Blend protein shake on high for about 60 seconds or until smooth.
4. Option to add more almond milk as needed to thin out your smoothie.
5. Serve immediately.

NUTRITION FACTS

Serving Size: 1/2 Calories: 220 Sugar: 9 Sodium: 147 Fat: 10 Carbohydrates: 23 Fiber: 4 Protein: 15

111. MOCHA COFFEE SMOOTHIE

Prep Time: 10 minutes

Cook Time: 5 minutes

Total Time: 15 minutes

INGREDIENTS

- ¾ cup of brewed coffee cooled in the fridge
- One frozen banana
- One date pitted (or 1 tsp maple syrup)
- 1 tsp vanilla extract
- ¾ cup of frozen cauliflower
- 1/4 cup of unsweetened oat milk (or non-dairy milk), + more if necessary
- 1/2 tbsp cacao powder
- 1 serving Protein Smoothie Boost, optional

INSTRUCTIONS

1. Add all ingredients into the blender.
2. Blend on high until creamy.
3. Pour into a glass and enjoy immediately.

112. ICED COFFEE SMOOTHIE

Prep Time 5 minutes

Total Time 5 minutes

Ingredients

- 1 cup of ice cubes
- One frozen banana cut into chunks
- 1 cup of brewed coffee chilled
- 1 cup of milk of any kind
- ¼ cup of old-fashioned oats
- 1-2 tbsp honey
- 1 tsp vanilla bean paste or vanilla extract

Instructions

1. Blend the ice, banana, coffee, milk, oats, honey, and vanilla essence in a blender canister.

2. Blend until the desired consistency is achieved. To sweeten, add extra honey if necessary.
3. Immediately pour into a large glass and serve.

Nutrition

Serving: 1g | Calories: 309kcal | Carbohydrates: 58g | Protein: 8g | Fat: 6g | Saturated Fat: 3g | Cholesterol: 12mg | Sodium: 58mg | Potassium: 715mg | Fiber: 5g | Sugar: 32g | Vitamin A: 273IU | Vitamin C: 10mg | Calcium: 148mg | Iron: 1mg

113. PEANUT BUTTER COFFEE SMOOTHIE

PREP TIME 2 mins

COOK TIME 2 mins

TOTAL TIME 4 mins

INGREDIENTS

- ¼ Cup of Creamy Peanut Butter
- One ripe banana
- ½ cup of cold brew coffee
- ½ cup of almond milk vanilla
- ⅓ cup of quick oats
- ½ tsp. ground ginger
- 1 tsp. vanilla extract
- shaved

INSTRUCTIONS

1. Add all the ingredients into a high-quality blender and blend until creamy and smooth!
2. Simple and Delightful! Enjoy.

NUTRITION

Serving: 1Serving

Calories: 575kcal

Carbohydrates: 78g

Protein: 17g

Fat: 24g

Saturated Fat: 3g

Polyunsaturated Fat: 5g

Monounsaturated Fat: 7g

Sodium: 264mg

Potassium: 744mg

Fiber: 11g

Sugar: 23g

Vitamin A: 7IU

Vitamin C: 18mg

Calcium: 26mg

Iron: 19mg

114. COMPETITIVE COFFEE SMOOTHIE WITH DATES & BANANA

prep time: 5 minutes

cook time: 0 minutes

total time: 5 minutes

preparation

1. Also, I've been storing leftover coffee in a Mason jar in the fridge to always have cold coffee on hand to make this.
2. Also, every morning, I slice up a banana and put it in the freezer, so it's nice and calm when I get up.

115. I'M READY TO MAKE MY SMOOTHIE.

INGREDIENTS

- One banana, sliced and frozen

- 3/4 cup of leftover coffee
- 1/4 cup of almond milk
- 1 tbsp almond butter
- a handful of ice cubes
- 2 Medjool dates, pitted
- 1/4 cup of cauliflower; see notes above
- pinch sea salt, such as Maldon
- cacao nibs for sprinkling, optional

INSTRUCTIONS

1. Place all ingredients in a blender, and purée until smooth. Pour into a glass, and top with cacao nibs if you wish.

116. KETO COFFEE SMOOTHIE

PREP TIME:5 MINS

TOTAL TIME:5 MINS

INGREDIENTS

- 8 OuncesBrewed coffee chilled, stored in the fridge 1 hour
- ⅓ cup of Heavy Cream
- 2 tbsp Unsweetened Almond Milk
- 1 tbsp Almond butter
- 1 tsp Vanilla Extract
- 2-3 tbsperythritol use 2 tbsp only if your collagen protein powder is already sweetened with sugar-free sweetener
- 1 cup of ice cubes - add up to 1/4 cup of extra for an ultra frothy smoothie
- 1 tbsp Collagen Protein Powder – optional

INSTRUCTIONS

2. Make fresh coffee and measure 8 oz. before beginning the recipe. Set aside for 1 hour or overnight in the refrigerator. You can also use 2 tsp instant coffee dissolved in 8 oz boiling water, cooled in the fridge like brewed coffee, and then used in the recipe.

3. Cold-brewed coffee, unsweetened almond milk, heavy cream, almond butter (or MCT oil), vanilla, collagen protein powder (some contain additional sweetness, so watch out), erythritol, and 3/4 cup ice cubes in a blender
4. Blend on high until frothy, taste, and adjust sweetness as needed, adding a pinch of erythritol or 1/4 extra ice cubes for a frothier smoothie if required.
5. To combine the new components, blend on high speed one more.

NUTRITION FACTS

AMOUNT PER SERVING (1 SMOOTHIE)

CALORIES 320.2CALORIES FROM FAT 288

% DAILY VALUE*

FAT 32g49%

Saturated Fat 14.6g91%

CHOLESTEROL 81.5mg27%

SODIUM 130.8mg6%

POTASSIUM 313.5mg9%

CARBOHYDRATES 6.4g2%

Fiber 2.5g10%

118. THIS HEALTHY CHOCOLATE COFFEE PROTEIN SMOOTHIE.

INGREDIENTS

- Two chopped frozen bananas
- One scoop chocolate protein powder
- 1 cup of brewed coffee
- ½ cup of low-fat vanilla yogurt
- ½ tsp vanilla extract

INSTRUCTIONS

1. Add all ingredients into a blender (affiliate link) and blend until smooth. Add milk or water to thin if desired.

Nutrition Facts

Serving Size 1.5 cups of

Serves 2

Amount Per Serving

Calories 332

% Daily Value*

Total Fat 1.9g   2%

Cholesterol 10.8mg   4%

Sodium 119.7mg   5%

Total Carbohydrate 38.6g   14%

Sugars 23g

119. COLD BREW COFFEE BANANA SMOOTHIE

Prep Time 5 mins

Total Time 5 mins

Ingredients

- Two bananas
- ½ cup of vanilla almond milk
- 2 tbsp almond butter
- One pinch cinnamon
- 1 tbsp flax seed (whole or ground)
- 1 cup of ice
- 2-3 Ounces concentrated cold brew coffee

Instructions

2. In a blender, combine all of the ingredients. To break up the ice, pulse 2-3 times, then blend until smooth and creamy. Pour into a glass or a travel tumbler and drink right away!

Nutrition Facts

Cold Brew Coffee Banana Smoothie

Amount Per Serving

Calories 238Calories from Fat 108

% Daily Value*

Fat 12g18%

Sodium 85mg4%

120. BLUEBERRY COFFEE BREAKFAST SMOOTHIE

Prep Time1 min

Total Time2 mins

Ingredients

- ½ cup of Rolled Oats (90 grams)
- 1 cup of Fresh Blueberries (125 grams)
- 2 tsp Instant Coffee
- 6 Dates, pitted
- 1 cup of Almond Milk (250 ml)

Instructions

3. Mix the oats, blueberries (rinsed), instant coffee, dates, and milk in a blender.
4. Process until smooth.
5. Serve right away!

Nutrition Facts

Blueberry Coffee Breakfast Smoothie

Amount per Serving

Calories 199

% Daily Value*

Fa3 g

Sodium

165 mg

Potassium 303 mg

121. EASY BANANA SPINACH SMOOTHIE

PREP TIME 5 mins

TOTAL TIME 5 mins

INGREDIENTS

- 1 tbsp almond butter
- ⅔ cup of Greek yogurt
- ½ banana
- ¾ cup of water
- One scoop vanilla protein powder
- One huge handful of spinal instructions

NUTRITION

Serving: 12ouncesCalories: 365kcalCarbohydrates: 26gProtein: 46gFat: 10gSaturated Fat: 1gPolyunsaturated Fat: 8gCholesterol: 13mgSodium: 153mgFiber: 6gSugar: 13g

122. GREEN PROTEIN POWER BREAKFAST SMOOTHIE

Prep Time: 5 minutes

Total Time: 5 minutes

INGREDIENTS

- 1 cup of (250 ml) unsweetened almond milk
- One ripe banana, frozen
- ½ cup of (125 ml) chopped mango, frozen
- 1-2 large handfuls of baby spinach
- ¼ cup of (60 ml) pumpkin seeds (pepita seeds)
- 2 tbsp (30 ml) hemp hearts (hulled hemp seeds)

- optional: ½ scoop (approx. 30ml) vanilla protein powder + ¼ cup of (60ml) water

INSTRUCTIONS

1. Layer the spinach, banana, mango, pumpkin seeds, and hemp hearts in a blender (or a large tumbler if using an immersion blender). Blend in the almond milk until the pumpkin seeds are entirely smooth. This recipe yields a single large smoothie (2 cups or - 500ml).

123. CREAMY, COFFEE PROTEIN SMOOTHIE

Ingredients

- 3/4 cup of cold, brewed coffee
- 1/4 cup of skim milk
- 1/2 cup of Greek yogurt, vanilla flavored
- Four dates
- 2 tbsp whey protein powder, vanilla
- 1 cup of ice

Instructions

2. Put the Greek yogurt, dates, protein powder, and milk in a high-powered blender and process until the dates are chopped into small pieces.
3. Add the coffee and ice, then process until smooth and creamy.

Nutrition Facts:

240 calories, 39 g carbohydrates, 2 g fiber, 32 g sugars, 1 g fat, 0 g saturated fat, 5 mg cholesterol, 21 g protein, 100 mg sodium, 20% DV for calcium, 15% DV for potassium, 6% DV for Vitamin D

124. SUMMERLICIOUS FRUIT SMOOTHIES

Prep Time: 15 min

Total Time: 15 minute

INGREDIENTS

- Ouncesor 1 cup of) old-fashioned oats
- 860ml (3 1/3 + 1/4 cups of) part skimmed milk
- 150ml (almost 2/3 cup of) water
- Two large bananas (about 195g or 14oz every), peeled and chopped
- One large pineapple (about 1.7kg or 3.7 pounds), peeled and chopped (yield about 700g or 1.5 pounds)
- 340g (12 Ouncesor nine apricots) apricots, pitted
- 335g (12 Ounces) cherries, pitted
- 320g (11.3 Ouncesor 1 cup of 2 TBSP) frozen blueberries

BLUEBERRY BANANA

- 25g (1/4 cup of) old-fashioned oats
- 200ml (1/2 + 1/3 cup of) milk
- 2/3 large banana, chopped
- 90g (5 TBSP) frozen blueberries
- PINEAPPLE APRICOT
- 50ml (almost 1/4 cup of) water
- 260g (roughly 9 Ounces) chopped pineapple
- 100g (3.5 Ounces) pitted apricots (2 1/2 apricots)

PINEAPPLE BANANA

- 120ml (1/2 cup of) milk
- 180g (6.3 Ounces) chopped pineapple
- One banana, chopped
- APRICOT BLUEBERRY
- 180ml (3/4 cup of) milk
- 100g (3.5 Ounces) frozen blueberries
- 85g (3 Ounces) pitted apricots (about two apricots)
- 1/3 large banana

CHERRY APRICOT

- 25g (1/4 cup of) old-fashioned oats
- 180ml (3/4 cup of) milk
- 100g (3.5 Ounces) pitted cherries
- 70g (2.5 Ounces) pitted apricots (about two apricots)

FRUITY MIX

- 100ml (almost 1/2 cup of) water

- 40g (1.4 Ounces) pitted cherries
- 40g (1.4 oz) pitted apricots (1 apricot)
- 50g (1.8 Ounces) frozen blueberries
- 100g (3.5 Ounces) chopped pineapple

CHERRY BERRY OAT

- 50g (1/2 cup of) old-fashioned oats
- 180ml (3/4 cup of) milk
- 80g (2.8 Ounces) pitted cherries
- 80g (2.8 Ounces) frozen blueberries

Instructions

1. Prepare all of the fruit first. Rinse thoroughly, then peel the bananas and pineapple, as well as the cherries and apricots. The blueberries do not need to be thawed.
2. When making an oat smoothie, start by putting the oats in the blender and blending them until they become a powder. Then, unless you plan to freeze the grains and fruit together, you can combine everything simultaneously.
3. The liquids and the rest of the fruit are then added.
4. Every smoothie should be blended for about a minute or until all of the large chunks of fruit are pureed. Then, taste and see if anything more needs to be added.
5. Have fun!

125. ENERGIZING GREEN SMOOTHIE

PREP TIME 5 minutes

TOTAL TIME 5 minutes

Ingredients

- 2 cups of fresh spinach
- 2 cups of water
- 1 cup of frozen mango
- 1 cup of frozen pineapple
- Two bananas
- 2 Tbsp chia seeds

Instructions

1. In a blender, combine spinach and water. Blend until all of the leafy bits are gone.
2. Mango, pineapple, bananas, and chia seeds are all good additions. Blend until completely smooth.
3. Serve and enjoy!

Nutrition Information:

Amount Per Serving: CALORIES: 163TOTAL FAT: 2gSATURATED FAT: 0gTRANS FAT: 0gUNSATURATED FAT: 2gCHOLESTEROL: 0mgSODIUM: 20mgCARBOHYDRATES: 36gFIBER: 5gSUGAR: 26gPROTEIN: 3g

126.BULLETPROOF COFFEE RECIPE

INGREDIENTS:

- 1 cup of Bulletproof coffee (brewed)
- 1 tsp. to 2 tbsp. Brain Octane C8 MCT oil
- 1-2 tbsp. Grass-fed, unsalted butter or 1-2 tsp. Grass-Fed Ghee
- Bulletproof tip: If you're new to MCT oil, start with 1 tsp. and build up to the full serving size over several days. You can also adjust the amount of butter (or Ghee) to find what works for you.

INSTRUCTIONS:

1. Bulletproof coffee beans should be used to make 1 cup (8-12 ounces) of coffee.
2. In a blender, combine the coffee, Brain Octane C8 MCT oil, and butter or Ghee.
3. Blend for 20-30 seconds, or until the mixture resembles a creamy latte. Have fun!
4. If you don't have a blender, combine all of the ingredients in a large mug and whisk with a milk frother until smooth and creamy.
5. 1 cup (about)

NUTRITIONAL INFORMATION

(1 CUP OF):

Calories: 230

Fat: 25g

Saturated Fat: 21g

Carbs: 0g

Protein: 0g

Fiber: 0g

Sugar: 0g

Salt: 0mg

127. CHOCOLATE ALMOND COFFEE SMOOTHIE

INGREDIENTS

- 1 tsp. chia seeds
- 1 tsp. instant espresso powder
- 1 cup of chocolate almond milk, cold
- 1/2 cup of fresh spinach leaves
- One medium peeled and chopped banana, frozen
- 1 tbsp almond butter

INSTRUCTIONS

1. In a blender, mix the chia seeds and instant espresso powder. Pour about 1/4 cup of chocolate almond milk into the mixture. Allow 5-10 minutes for this mixture to rest.
2. Mix the spinach leaves, frozen banana, almond butter, and the leftover chocolate almond milk in a blender. Blend on high speed until completely smooth. Immediately pour into a glass and serve.

128. BASIC GREEN SMOOTHIE RECIPE

INGREDIENTS

- 1 cup of milk (see this page for a listing of homemade non-dairy milk)
- One banana
- 2 cups of fresh spinach
- 1 tbsp flax seed (optional)

INSTRUCTIONS

1. Place all ingredients in a blender, and blend on high until smooth.

2. Add ice cubes to the blender if you want it extra cold and thick. Or use a frozen banana / frozen mango in place of ice.

129. PERFECT CELERY SMOOTHIE

Prep Time: 5 minutes

Ingredients

- Four medium stalks celery (¾ cup of chopped)
- One large green apple
- One banana
- ½ tsp peeled and grated ginger (from fresh ginger root)
- 2 cups of baby spinach leaves
- ½ cup of water
- Ten ice cubes
- 1 ½ tbsp fresh squeezed lemon juice (1/2 lemon)

Instructions

1. Chop the celery into small pieces. Take the peel from the apple and chop it into bits. Cut the banana into small pieces. Ginger should be peeled and grated or minced.
2. In a blender, combine all of the ingredients and blend until smooth, stopping and scraping as needed and adding a splash of water if the mixture is too thick. Drink right away or keep in the fridge for up to a day.

130. RED BEET SMOOTHIE

Total Time: 10 minutes

Prep Time: 10 minutes

INGREDIENTS

- One small red beet, trimmed and peeled
- One large apple, cored
- One stalk of celery
- 1 cup of carrot juice
- 1 cup of almond milk
- 2/3 cup of frozen sliced every
- 1-inch piece of ginger, peeled and sliced

INSTRUCTIONS

1. Cut the beet, apple, and celery into small pieces.
2. In a blender, combine all the ingredients and blend until smooth. Taste the smoothie to check if it's sweet enough for you. If you want it to be a little sweeter, add a little extra fruit. Serve right away. Smoothie can be stored in a jar for up to 2 days.

NUTRITION INFORMATION:

Amount per drink: Calories: 169, Total Fat 2g, Saturated Fat: 0.5g, Sodium: 213mg, Cholesterol: 0mg, Total Carbohydrate: 38g, Dietary Fiber: 7g, Sugar: 24g, Protein 4g

131. STRAWBERRY BANANA SMOOTHIE {MADE WITH ALMOND BREEZE}

Prep Time 3 minutes

Total Time 3 minutes

Ingredients

- One banana medium-sized
- 1 1/2 cups of frozen strawberries (5 ounces measured on a food scale)
- 1/3 cup of plain Greek yogurt
- 1/2 cup of almond milk

Instructions

1. Blend all of the ingredients in a blender until smooth.
2. Add a few more frozen strawberries and blend again if the mixture appears to be too thin. If the sauce is too thick, add a splash of milk.

132. COFFEE PROTEIN SHAKE

PREP TIME 5 mins

TOTAL TIME 5 mins

INGREDIENTS

- ½ cup of cold double brewed coffee see notes below
- One large frozen banana
- ½ cup of vanilla almond milk
- ½ cup of vanilla Greek yogurt
- ½ tbsp cocoa powder

INSTRUCTIONS

1. In a blender, combine the almond milk, coffee, frozen banana, vanilla Greek yogurt, and chocolate powder.
2. Blend for 1 minute, or until smooth and well combined.
3. Smoothie should have a thick, icy texture. If the smoothie isn't wide enough, add 4-5 ice cubes and combine again.
4. Serve right away.

NUTRITION

Calories: 285kcal

133. STRAWBERRY BANANA SMOOTHIE RECIPE

PREP TIME: 5 mins

TOTAL TIME: 5 mins

INGREDIENTS

- 2 cups of fresh strawberries, halved
- One banana, quartered and frozen
- 1/2 cup of Greek yogurt
- 1/2 cup of milk

INSTRUCTIONS

1. Blend all of the ingredients in a high-powered blender until smooth.
2. LISA'S TIPS Although Greek yogurt is thicker; regular yogurt could be used in this recipe.

3. Using a Vitamix blender, The Vitamix Ascent 3500 is what I use, and I love it!
4. Instead of plastic straws, I also propose these stainless steel and glass straws.

NUTRITION

CALORIES: 198.1kcal, CARBOHYDRATES: 30.8g, PROTEIN: 5.9g, FAT: 7.1g, SATURATED FAT: 3.7g, CHOLESTEROL: 21.2mg, SODIUM: 66.6mg, FIBER: 4.8g, SUGAR: 20.5g

134.3 INGREDIENT STRAWBERRY BANANA SMOOTHIE

Cook Time: 5 minutes

Total Time: 5 minutes

Ingredients

- One ripe banana sliced about 1/2 cup of
- 10 ounces frozen sliced strawberries you can also use fresh
- 1/2 cup of milk

Instructions

1. Place the strawberries, bananas, and milk in a blender. Puree until smooth and creamy.

135.THE BEST STRAWBERRY BANANA SMOOTHIE

Prep Time: 5 minutes

Cook Time: 0

Total Time: 6 minutes

Ingredients

- 2 ½ cups of frozen strawberries
- Two ripe bananas (no green bananas)
- One ¼ cup of milk (cow, almond, soy, oat)
- 5 oz plain Greek yogurt
- 2 tbsp honey

Instructions

2. In a blender, combine all of the ingredients in the order indicated above, then blend until smooth, about 45 to 60 seconds.
3. Serve right away.

Nutrition

Calories: 320kcal | Carbohydrates: 68g | Protein: 15g | Fat: 1g | Saturated Fat: 1g | Cholesterol: 7mg | Sodium: 94mg | Potassium: 1037mg | Fiber: 7g | Sugar: 51g | Vitamin A: 388IU | Vitamin C: 116mg | Calcium: 299mg | Iron: 1mg

136. GREEK YOGURT SMOOTHIE

PREP: 3 mins

COOK: 2 mins

TOTAL: 5 mins

Ingredients

- 1 cup of whole frozen strawberries about ten large berries or mixed berries of choice
- One medium ripe banana peeled and cut in half
- ¾ cup of nonfat plain Greek yogurt
- 2 tbsp oatmeal
- 1 tbsp peanut butter or almond butter
- 1 to 2 tsp honey
- Water or unsweetened almond milk as needed
- Ice optional

Instructions

1. In a blender, combine strawberries, banana, Greek yogurt, oats, peanut butter, and one teaspoon of honey, except for the ice.
2. Blend until completely smooth. You may need to pause your blender and scrape down the pitcher a couple of times, depending on the size and power of your blender. If the mixture is too thick to blend, add a splash of water or almond milk, stir to move the contents of the blender about, and mix again; if the mixture is too thin, add a few ice cubes blender and blend again. If you want the smoothie to be sweeter, taste it and add more honey if necessary. Finally, pour into a glass and take a sip!

Nutrition

SERVING: 1smoothieCALORIES: 392kcalCARBOHYDRATES: 57gPROTEIN: 25 gFAT: 10gSATURATED FAT: 2gCHOLESTEROL: 9mgPOTASSIUM: 997mgFIBER: 7gSUGAR: 35gVITAMIN A: 76IUVITAMIN C: 95mgCALCIUM: 218mgIRON: 1mg

137. KISS STRAWBERRY BANANA LEMON SMOOTHIE

Time 5 mins

Ingredients

- Three large or five medium strawberries, fresh or frozen
- 1/2 large banana, frozen
- 1/2 cup of milk of choice (almond, soy, etc.)
- One scoop of your favorite protein powder, if desired
- One generous squeeze of lemon juice

Instructions

1. Blend all of the ingredients in a Vitamix or high-powered blender on high until smooth, and the appropriate consistency is reached.
2. Consider adding 1-3 teaspoons of flax, chia, or hemp seeds for extra nutrients!

138. HIGH FIBER SMOOTHIE

Prep Time 5 mins

Total Time 5 mins

Ingredients

- 1 cup of frozen blueberries
- One whole overripe banana fresh or frozen
- 1 cup of fresh spinach
- 2/3 cup of 1% milk
- 1/3 cup of plain Greek yogurt
- 1-2 tbsp. honey or maple syrup
- 1 tbsp. ground flax seed

Instructions

1. Place all ingredients in a blender, puree until smooth.

Nutrition

Calories: 213kcal | Carbohydrates: 38g | Protein: 9g | Fat: 5g | Saturated Fat: 1g | Cholesterol: 6mg | Sodium: 62mg | Potassium: 581mg | Fiber: 6g | Sugar: 26g | Vitamin A: 1640IU | Vitamin C: 17mg | Calcium: 177mg | Iron: 1mg

139. PEVERYES & CREAM OATMEAL SMOOTHIE

prep time: 5 MINS

total time: 5 MINS

Ingredients

- ¾ cup of frozen every
- ½ cup of yogurt of choice
- ¼ cup ofSunsweet Prune Juice
- ¼ tsp cinnamon
- ¼ cup of rolled oats

Instructions

2. Add all ingredients to a blender and blend until smooth.
3. Serve and enjoy!

140. HIGH FIBER FRUIT AND VEGGIE SMOOTHIE

Prep Time 5 minutes

Ingredients

- 1 1/2 cups of fresh spinach (I use the packaged spinach because it's already washed)
- 3/4-1 cup of frozen strawberries
- 1/2 banana, frozen if possible
- 1 tbsp flax meal
- 1 tbsp toasted wheat germ, for gluten-free, leave this out and add 1 tbsp more of flax meal

- 1/2 tsp vanilla extract
- 3/4-1 cup of unsweetened vanilla almond milk, soy milk,
- 1/8 cup of cold water
- 1=2 drops all-natural Stevia, or one packet of Stevia, as need
- 1/2 cup of ice cubes

Instructions

1. 1.This is sooooo easy –
2. Place all ingredients in your blender and whirl up! That's it! Enjoy!!

141.BROCCOLI SMOOTHIE

Prep Time: 5 minutes

Ingredients

- 1 cup of cherries
- 1 cup of chopped broccoli
- One medium avocado
- One medium banana
- 1 tbsp flaxseed, ground
- 1 cup of pomegranate juice

Instructions

1. Blend all ingredients in a high-powered blender and drink!

142.AVOCADO PINEAPPLE HIGH FIBER SMOOTHIE

PREP TIME20 minutes

TOTAL TIME20 minutes

INGREDIENTS

- 1 cup of water or pineapple juice
- 1/2 frozen banana
- 1/2 avocado
- 1 cup of fresh pineapple chunks
- 1 tbsp of chia seeds
- Tip: You can add MiraLAX® for relief of occasional constipation.

INSTRUCTIONS

2. Add everything to the blender.
3. Blend for about 35 seconds or until well blended.
4. You can add more water or juice if it is too thick.

143. THE BEST LOW CARB GREEN SMOOTHIE

Prep Time 5 mins

Ingredients

- ¼ cup of frozen banana
- 1 ½ cups of fresh spinach
- 2 tbsp chia seeds
- ½ tsp vanilla extract
- 1 cup of unsweetened almond milk
- ¼ cup of plain Greek yogurt
- One scoop protein powder
- 4-5 ice cubes

Instructions

1. Add all ingredients to the blender and blend until smooth (about 1 minute).

144. ULTRA-SATISFYING STRAWBERRY BANANA SMOOTHIE RECIPE

INGREDIENTS

- One medium (125 grams) ripe banana, 1 cup of chopped
- One heaping cup of (150 grams) fresh or frozen strawberries
- 1 1/2 cups of (185 grams) chopped zucchini (about half a medium zucchini)
- 2 tbsp nut butter like peanut or almond butter, see our homemade peanut butter recipe
- 1 tbsp chia seeds
- Pinch ground cinnamon
- Pinch sea salt
- 1 cup of water or milk (dairy or non-dairy)
- Honey, agave, or other sweeteners as needed

DIRECTIONS

2. In a high-powered blender, combine the banana, strawberries, zucchini, nut butter, chia seeds, cinnamon, salt, and water. Blend on high until smooth and creamy. Taste and adjust with a little sweetener if necessary. If the smoothie isn't mixing well or appears to be overly thick, add a splash of liquid and blend until smooth.

3. Divide the mixture between two glasses (or add to one tall glass for a double serving). Before serving, garnish with more chia seeds and diced strawberries if desired.

145. APPLE-BERRY COLLAGEN SMOOTHIE

PREP TIME5 mins

TOTAL TIME5 mins

INGREDIENTS

- One granny smith apple (cored and chopped)
- ½ cup of frozen
- 1 cup of fresh
- 1 tbsp chia seeds
- Two scoops of collagen peptides (unflavored)
- ¾ cup of nut milk
- 1-2 cups of ice

INSTRUCTIONS

1. Put all ingredients in a blender and puree until smooth

NUTRITION

Calories: 299kcalCarbohydrates: 56gProtein: 23gFat: 6gSaturated Fat: 1gPolyunsaturated Fat: 3gSodium: 192mgPotassium: 346mgFiber: 14gSugar: 38gVitamin A: 400IUVitamin C: 77.6mgCalcium: 400mgIron: 2.5mg

146. CHOCOLATE FIBER SMOOTHIE CUBES

Prep Time: 30 minutes

Total Time: 30 minutes

INGREDIENTS

- 4 cups of unsweetened almond milk, + more if needed
- 1/2 cup of chia seeds
- 1 cup of shelled hemp hearts
- 8 tsp psyllium husk powder
- 4 tbsp cacao powder
- Eight soft, Medjool dates, pitted
- 2 tsp pure vanilla extract
- Big pinch sea salt

INSTRUCTIONS

2. In a mixing bowl, combine 2 cups almond milk and chia seeds and whisk thoroughly. Allow for 10-15 minutes of resting time.
3. Fill a blender jar halfway with chia gel. Combine the remaining ingredients. Puree until completely smooth. If necessary, add a bit of additional liquid to make blending easier. The consistency of the mixture will be thick and pudding-like.
4. Fill two 16-well ice cube trays halfway with the mixture. It's OK if the mixture slightly overflows the wells, as long as it doesn't spill over the trays' sides.
5. Freeze the trays overnight or until they are excellent. Place the cubes in an airtight, freezer-safe container after removing them from the trays. Store for up to 2 weeks in the freezer or a little longer if using a deep freezer.

147. DETOX GREEN SMOOTHIE
INGREDIENTS

- One banana (preferably frozen, in slices)
- 1 cup of frozen pineapple chunks
- 1 cup ofevery piece (can be frozen)
- 1/2 cup of Greek yogurt (Vanilla, plain, etc.)
- 2 cups of spinach
- 3/4 cup of water, apple juice,
- Juice and zest of 1 lime

- Optional: 1 tbsp ground flaxseed and chia seeds, 1 tsp freshly grated ginger and cinnamon.

INSTRUCTIONS

1. Place all ingredients in a blender and blend until smooth and creamy. Add more liquid if needed to help it mix well.

148. HIGH-FIBER KALE AND APPLE DETOX SMOOTHIE FOR HEALTHY DIGESTION

Total Time: 5 minutes

Ingredients

- 1 cup of chopped kale
- 1 cup of chopped spinach
- One celery stick, chopped
- 1 Granny Smith apple, sliced
- ½ medium cucumber, peeled and chopped
- 1 tbsp lemon juice
- 1 tbsp honey or as need
- 1 cup of water
- 1 cup of ice

Instructions

2. Place all the ingredients in a blender and blend until smooth.
3. Serve immediately.

149. SLIMMING GREEN SMOOTHIE

Ingredients

- 2 cups of spinach
- One stalk celery
- One orange
- One banana
- One scoop flavorless protein optional
- One lime

- 1 1/2 cups of pineapple
- ice to preference
- water to achieve thickness preference 1-2 cups of

Instructions

1. Put everything in your blender and blend until smooth
2. Add ice and water to achieve desired consistency

Nutrition

Calories: 83kcal | Carbohydrates: 21g | Protein: 1g | Sodium: 21mg | Potassium: 359mg | Fiber: 3g | Sugar: 13g | Vitamin A: 1580IU | Vitamin C: 59mg | Calcium: 46mg | Iron: 0.8mg

150. HIGH FIBER BLUEBERRY KALE SMOOTHIE

PREP TIME 2 minutes

COOK TIME 2 minutes

Ingredients

- send a grocery list
- 1/2 cup of frozen blueberries (rinsed)
- 1 tbsp Bow Hill Organic Heirloom Blueberry Powder
- 1 tbsp ground flax seed
- 1/2 frozen banana
- 1 cup of fresh kale (rinsed)
- 2/3 cup of almond milk

Directions

1. Add all ingredients to a blender and blend until smooth.
2. Pour into a glass.

151. MIXED BERRY SMOOTHIE

Prep Time: 5 minutes

INGREDIENTS

- 3/4 cup of Ocean Spray Light Cranberry Juice Drink, any flavor
- 3/4 cup of frozen mixed berries (strawberries, raspberries, blackberries, and blueberries)
- One 6-ounce container low fat berry-flavored yogurt
- 1/2 banana, cut into slices
- Nutrition InfoNutritional Info

DIRECTIONS

1. Mix all ingredients in a blender. Blend for a few seconds on high speed or until ingredients are thoroughly mixed. Pour into a large glass.

152. FIVE-INGREDIENT GO-TO GREEN SMOOTHIE

PREP TIME: 5 MINS

TOTAL TIME: 5 MINS

Ingredients

- 1-1/2 cups of ice
- One medium banana, fresh
- Two handfuls of spinach
- ½ avocado
- 1 ½-2 cups of milk of choice
- Two scoops of protein powder of choice (such as collagen peptides)

Instructions

2. Place all ingredients into a blender.
3. Blend until smooth and creamy, and no chunks remain.
4. Serve and enjoy

Nutrition

SERVING SIZE: 1/2 OF RECIPE

CALORIES: 215

SUGAR: 7 G

SODIUM: 180 MG

FAT: 8 G

CARBOHYDRATES: 22 G

FIBER: 7 G

PROTEIN: 13 G

153. EVERY BANANA FLAX SMOOTHIE

INGREDIENTS

- 1/2 cup of plain
- 1/2 cup of cold water
- 3-4 frozen banana chunks
- One every
- 1 tbsp flax seeds
- 1 tbsp nutritional yeast (less if you are new to this flavor)
- 1 tsp honey, optional

INSTRUCTIONS

1. Mix all in a blender and process until smooth and creamy.

NUTRITION

Calories: 292

Sugar: 35

Fat: 4.8

Carbohydrates: 48

Protein: 14

154. 3-INGREDIENT BERRY SMOOTHIE

Prep Time 7 mins

Total Time 7 mins

INGREDIENTS

One frozen banana

1 1/2 cup of frozen berries (I used raspberry, blueberry, strawberry)

1/4 cup of water or your choice of milk

INSTRUCTIONS

2. Blend all the ingredients of the smoothie until smooth. Then, add more or less liquid to suit your tastes.
3. Serve in a bowl and top with the chopped fruit.

155.3 VEGGIE-PACKED SMOOTHIES FOR BEGINNERS

prep time: 5 MINS

cook time: 0 MINUTES

total time: 5 MINS

Ingredients

- 1/2 cup of raspberries (frozen)
- 1/2 cup of strawberries
- 1/2 cup of cauliflower (*steamed for easier digestion)
- One 1-inch cube of ginger
- 1 cup of nut milk (I use almond milk)

DAILY GREENS SMOOTHIE

- 1/2 cup of spinach
- 1/4 avocado
- 1/2 banana (frozen)
- 1 tbsp hemp hearts
- 1 tsp chia seeds
- 1 cup of nut milk

NUTTY BANANA SMOOTHIE

One banana (frozen)

1/2 cup of zucchini, skin removed and chopped into cubes

2 tbsp almond butter

1/2 tsp cinnamon

1 cup of nut milk (or light coconut milk)

Instructions

1. For every smoothie, add all ingredients to a blender and blend until smooth.
2. Drink right away and enjoy!

156. GLOWING GREEN SMOOTHIE

Total Time: 11 Minutes

Ingredients

- 1½ cup of (360 ml) water
- ¾ pound (340 g) romaine lettuce
- 1½ cup of (45 g) baby spinach
- 3 (205 g) celery stalk
- 1 (120 g) apple, cored, halved
- 1 (120 g) pear, cored, halved
- 1 (110 g) banana, peeled
- ½ lemon, peeled

Directions

1. Put all of the ingredients in the Vitamix container in the order stated, then close the lid.
2. Start the machine at the lowest setting and gradually increase to the highest setting.
3. Blend for 45 seconds or until smooth, scraping down the sides with a tamper as needed.

Notes

Add cilantro and parsley leaves to this smoothie for added flavor. Then, start blending and add more components through the lid plug while mixing if all the details don't fit into the container.

157. BANANA SPINACH SMOOTHIE

PREP TIME 1 minute

TOTAL TIME 1 minute

Ingredients:

- Half a large or one small very ripe banana
- 1 cup of milk (or dairy substitute)
- 2 cups of fresh baby spinach

Instructions:

1. Toss everything in a blender with a few ice cubes.
2. Blend and enjoy!
3.

158. HEALTHY RED AND GREEN SMOOTHIE

Prep Time: 10 Min

Cook Time: 0 min

INGREDIENTS

- 1 cup of frozen mango
- 1/2 frozen banana
- 1/2-3/4 cup of soy milk
- Handful fresh baby spinach
- 1/4 tsp ground ginger

- 1 cup of frozen red raspberries
- 1/3 cup of pomegranate-cherry juice
- One blood orange.

INSTRUCTIONS

1. In a blender cup, purée all of the ingredients for the green layer until smooth. Eliminate from the equation.
2. In a blender cup, purée all of the ingredients for the red layer until smooth.
3. Divide the red and green smoothie mixture between two glasses to serve.

NUTRITION

Serving Size: 1/2 recipe

Calories: 310 kcals

Sugar: 33 g

Sodium: 70 mg

Fat: 9 g

Saturated Fat: 1.5 g

Unsaturated Fat: 7.5 g

Trans Fat: 0 g

159. ALKALINE SMOOTHIE

Prep Time: 3 mins

Cook Time: 2 mins

Total Time: 5 mins

Ingredients

- 1 cup of almond milk
- 1 cup of watermelon cubed

- Five strawberries frozen
- 1/2 small banana
- One handful of spinach fresh
- 1 tsp chia seeds
- 1 cup of ice

Instructions

1. In a blender, combine the ingredients in the order stated.
2. Blend the smoothie until it is well combined.
3. Mix the greens with the banana, chia seeds, half of the ice, and half of the almond milk to avoid a brown smoothie.
4. Then, in a blender, combine the watermelon strawberries, almond milk, and ice.
5. Combine the smoothies in a single glass and serve.

Nutrition

Nutrition Facts

Alkaline Smoothie

Amount Per Serving

160. CARROT GINGER TURMERIC SMOOTHIE

PREP TIME 20 minutes

TOTAL TIME 20 minutes

Ingredients
CARROT JUICE

- 2 cups of carrots
- 1 1/2 cups of filtered water

SMOOTHIE

- One large ripe banana (previously peeled, sliced, and frozen // more for a sweeter smoothie)
- 1 cup of frozen or fresh pineapple
- 1/2 Tbsp fresh ginger (peeled // 1 small knob yields ~1/2 Tbsp)

- 1/4 tsp ground turmeric (or sub cinnamon)
- 1/2 cup of carrot juice
- 1 Tbsp lemon juice (1/2 small lemon yields ~1 Tbsp or 15 ml)
- 1 cup of unsweetened almond milk

Instructions

1. Carrot juice is made by blending carrots and filtered water in a high-powered blender until totally pureed and smooth. If it's not integrating well, add extra water and scrape down the sides as needed.
2. Pour the juice over a big, thin dishcloth draped over a mixing basin. Then, lifting on the towel's corners, start twisting and squeezing the juice out until all of it is gone. The pulp can be saved for smoothies or baked goods (such as carrot muffins).
3. Transfer the carrot juice to a mason jar; it will last for several days, but it is best when it is fresh.
4. Blend the smoothie ingredients in a high-powered blender until creamy and smooth. If it's not blending well, add extra carrot juice or almond milk. Scrape down the sides if necessary.
5. Taste and modify the flavors as needed, adding extra banana or pineapple for sweetness, lemon for acidity, ginger for bite, and turmeric for warmth if desired.

Nutrition

(1 of 2 servings)

Serving: 1 smoothiesCalories: 144Carbohydrates: 32 gProtein: 2.4 gFat: 2.3 gSaturated Fat: 0 gTrans Fat: 0 gCholesterol: 0 mgSodium: 112 mgFiber: 5 gSugar: 17.5 g

161. ANTIOXIDANT-RICH BLUEBERRY SMOOTHIE

Prep Time: 5 minutes

Total Time: 5 minutes

Ingredients

- 1 cup of original almond milk or water
- 1 Tbsp chia seeds
- One banana peeled

- Two oranges
- 2 cups of frozen blueberries

Instructions

1. IN A BLENDER, COMBINE EVERYTHING IN THE ORDER SPECIFIED (1 CUP ALMOND MILK, 1 TABLESPOON CHIA SEEDS, 1 BANANA, 2 ORANGES, AND 2 CUPS FROZEN BLUEBERRIES) AND SEASON TO TASTE. Then, PUSH THE SMOOTHIE BUTTON ON YOUR BLENDTEC AND WATCH IT GO!

162. KETO LOW CARB SMOOTHIE WITH ALMOND MILK

INGREDIENTS

- 1 Cup of Almond Breeze Original Almondmilk
- 1 Cup of Crushed ice
- 1/4 Cup of Avocado (about 1/2 an avocado or 60g)
- 3 Tbsp Monkfruit, or as need
- 2 Tbsp Natural creamy peanut butter (Almond butter for paleo)
- 1 Tbsp Unsweetened cocoa powder
- Get IngredientsPowered by Chicory

INSTRUCTIONS

2. Place all ingredients into a blender and blend until smooth.

163. APPLE POMEGRANATE SMOOTHIE BOWL RECIPE

Ingredients

- Apple - 1 cut in big pieces
- Pomegranate Seeds - 1/2 cup of + to garnish
- Instant Oats or quick oats - 1/3 cup of
- Peanut Butter - 1 tbsp
- Milk - 2 cups of
- Chocos - to garnish
- Honey/Sugar - as need optional

Instructions

3. BLEND THE APPLE, POMEGRANATE SEEDS, OATS, PEANUT BUTTER, AND MILK IN A BLENDER.
4. If desired, sweeten with honey or sugar. Blend until completely smooth.
5. Pour everything into the bowl.

164. HARLEY PASTERNAK BREAKFAST SMOOTHIE

INGREDIENTS

- One red apple
- One banana
- 3/4 cup of nonfat Greek yogurt
- 1/2 cup of nonfat milk
- 1/4 tsp cinnamon

DIRECTIONS

1. In a blender, combine all of the ingredients. (Depending on your blender's power, you might need to chop the apple and almonds into tiny bits before blending.)
2. Blend for 30 seconds on medium-high (or until desired consistency).

165. THE ULTIMATE LACTATION SMOOTHIE RECIPE

Ingredients

- 2 cups of almond milk
- 1/2 banana
- 1/2 cup of spinach
- 1 tbsp almond butter
- 1 tsp chia seed
- 1 tsp flaxseed

Preparation

1. Place the pineapple pieces flat in a resealable plastic bag. Freeze for at least 3 hours until solid.
2. Before measuring, shake the cans of coconut cream and coconut milk. In a blender, puree pineapple, coconut cream, coconut milk, white

rum, lime juice, and 3 cups ice (approximately 15 oz.) until smooth. Freeze the blender cup until the mixture has thickened (it should be the consistency of a milkshake), about 25–35 minutes.
3. Blend until the mixture has the consistency of a mushy frozen drink. Divide the mixture among the glasses. If using, add 12 oz. Dark rum to each and garnish with a cherry and lime wedge.

4. Make-Ahead: Pineapple can be cut up to three months ahead of time. Keep frozen till ready to use.
5. WATCH

166. CARROT BEETROOT JUICE WITH APPLES AND CELERY

Prep Time 10 mins

Total Time 10 mins

Ingredients

- Two apples
- One beet peeled
- Five carrots peeled
- Five celery stalks
- small piece of black radish peeled (about the size of the beet) (or use a 2-inch piece of ginger, peeled)

Instructions

1. Depending on the size of the juicer, cut vegetables and apples to make sure they fit through the feed chute.
2. Turn on the juicer and add vegetables and apples. Enjoy!

Nutrition Facts

Carrot Beetroot Juice with Apples and Celery

Amount Per Serving

Calories 190

% Daily Value*

Sodium 219mg10%

Potassium 1075mg31%

Carbohydrates 46g15%

167. COCONUT WATER SMOOTHIE

Prep Time: 5 minutes

Total Time: 5 minutes

Ingredients

- 1 ½ cups of pure coconut water
- One ripe banana
- 1 cup of frozen cranberries
- 1 cup of frozen blueberries
- 2 cups of loosely packed fresh spinach leaves
- 1 tbsp chia seeds
- ½ tsp ground cinnamon
- ¼ tsp ground ginger
- 2-3 ice cubes optional

Instructions

1. Place all ingredients in a high-speed blender and blend until smooth.
2. Enjoy!

168. HEALTHY GREEN SMOOTHIE

PREP TIME: 5 MINUTES

TOTAL TIME: 5 MINUTES

INGREDIENTS

- 1/2 cup of unsweetened coconut milk
- 1 1/2 tsp peeled and grated fresh ginger
- 1/2 cup of diced cucumber
- Two celery stalks, chopped
- 1 1/2 cups of chopped Swiss chard (about five leaves)
- 1/2 avocado, pit, and skin removed
- 3/4 cup of frozen pineapple

INSTRUCTIONS

1. In a blender, combine coconut milk and ginger.
2. Combine the cucumber, celery, Swiss chard, avocado, and pineapple in a mixing bowl.
3. Blend all of the ingredients until smooth, adding more coconut milk as needed to achieve the desired consistency. Take pleasure at the moment.

NUTRITION

SERVING SIZE: 16 ounces

CALORIES: 200

SUGAR: 13 g

SODIUM: 230 mg

FAT: 11 g

CARBOHYDRATES: 27 g

FIBER: 8 g

PROTEIN: 4 g

169. BEST TURMERIC SMOOTHIE

PREP TIME: 5 mins

TOTAL TIME: 5 mins

INGREDIENTS

- 1 cup of dairy-free milk
- 2 cups of frozen pineapple chunks
- One banana
- 1 tbsp fresh turmeric, grated
- 1 tsp fresh ginger, grated

INSTRUCTIONS

1. In a blender, combine all of the ingredients and blend on high for 30 seconds, or until creamy.
2. TIPS FROM LISA
3. The smoothie has a thick texture thanks to the frozen fruit, and it's pretty chilly and refreshing.

NUTRITION

CALORIES: 180kcal, CARBOHYDRATES: 41g, PROTEIN: 4g, FAT: 2g, SATURATED FAT: 1g, SODIUM: 34mg, POTASSIUM: 592mg, FIBER: 5g, SUGAR: 25g, VITAMIN A: 365iu, VITAMIN C: 89mg, CALCIUM: 110mg, IRON: 2mg

170. PEAR AND CINNAMON SMOOTHIE (DAIRY-FREE)

PREP TIME5 mins

TOTAL TIME5 mins

INGREDIENTS

- One pear, cored and chopped (ripe, soft pears work best)
- One banana, peeled and chopped
- 3-4 blocks (80g) frozen chopped spinach
- ¼ cup of (30g) gluten-free oats, millet flakes,
- ¼ cup of (70g) dairy-free plain yogurt
- 1 tsp cinnamon
- 200 ml dairy-free milk alternative or apple juice

INSTRUCTIONS

1. Add all the ingredients except the dairy-free milk alternative or apple juice to your blender.

171. ZUCCHINI SMOOTHIE RECIPE

PREP TIME 5 mins

TOTAL TIME 5 mins

INGREDIENTS

- 1 ½ cups of unsweetened almond milk
- 2 TBS vanilla protein powder
- ¼ tsp cinnamon
- 1 cup of zucchini
- 1 cup of spinach frozen
- ½ banana frozen
- ½ tsp pure vanilla extract

INSTRUCTIONS

2. Place the ingredients in the Vitamix Blender container in the order listed (or another high-powered blender).
3. Begin blending on low and gradually increase to high.
4. Blend for 30-50 seconds on high, or until the mixture is completely smooth.
5. (You can also use the smoothie software.)

NUTRITION

Serving: 1cup of

Calories: 137.2kcal

Carbohydrates: 17.3g

Protein: 12.5g

Fat: 3.8g

Polyunsaturated Fat: 0.4g

Monounsaturated Fat: 1.1g

Sodium: 205mg

Potassium: 540mg

Fiber: 5.5g

Sugar: 4.7g

Vitamin A: 2805IU

Vitamin C: 14.1mg

Calcium: 370mg

Iron: 3.2mg

172. WATERMELON STRAWBERRY SMOOTHIE

PREP TIME 2 mins

COOK TIME 0 mins

TOTAL TIME 2 mins

INGREDIENTS

- 1 cup of frozen strawberries
- 2 cups of frozen watermelon pieces seedless, cut into 1-inch cubes
- 1 cup of almond milk
- 2 tsp honey optional

INSTRUCTIONS

1. Add all the watermelon smoothie ingredients to the blender.
2. Blend the watermelon smoothie until smooth
3. Serve, and wash out your blender right away to avoid sticking.

NUTRITION

Calories: 99kcalCarbohydrates: 21gProtein: 1.9gFat: 1.7gSaturated Fat: 0.1gCholesterol: 0mgSodium: 73mgPotassium: 279mgFiber: 2gSugar: 15.9gCalcium: 22mgIron: 1mg

173. STRAWBERRY BANANA OAT SMOOTHIE

Prep 5 minutes

Ingredients

- 1 cup of unsweetened almond milk or 1% milk
- 1/2 cup of fat-free plain Greek yogurt
- 2 cups of (9 Ounces) frozen strawberries
- 1 1/2 ripe medium bananas
- 1/2 cup of quick oats or old fashioned oats
- 1 Tbsp honey
- 1/2 tsp vanilla extract

Instructions

1. Add all ingredients to a blender, cover, and blend until smooth. Serve immediately.

174. IMMUNITY BOOSTING SMOOTHIE RECIPE

Prep Time 5 mins

Total Time 5 mins

Ingredients

- One carrot, washed, peeled, and chopped into about five pieces
- One banana, peeled and chopped
- One whole clementine, peeled, segmented
- 1-inch knob fresh ginger, peeled and grated
- 6 to 8 ounces freshly squeezed orange juice
- 2 tbsp fresh lemon juice
- ¼ tsp turmeric powder
- ⅛ tsp ground cinnamon
- ⅓ cup of plain yogurt

- 1 cup of ice
- sweetener, optional

Instructions

2. In a high-powered blender, combine all ingredients in the order stated (sweetener is optional); blend until smooth.
3. Taste for sweetness and make adjustments as needed.

175. CASHEW APPLE GREEN SMOOTHIE

PREP TIME5 mins

COOK TIME5 mins

TOTAL TIME10 mins

INGREDIENTS

- 1/3 cup of raw unsalted cashews
- 1 cup of cold water, + more for soaking
- One organic ripe Fuji or gala apple cut into chunks, core discarded
- 1/2 banana, peeled and cut into chunks
- 2 cups of fresh organic baby spinach or baby kale (not mature kale-- baby kale is more tender and will blend up creamier)
- 16 ice cubes
- 1 tsp cinnamon
- 1/4 tsp nutmeg
- 1 tsp stevia or 1 tbsp agave nectar, or more as need (I use one packet of Truvia)

INSTRUCTIONS=

1. Add cashews to a small bowl half filled with cold water. Soak the cashews for at least 1 hour and up to 24 hours before using them (if soaking overnight, keep them refrigerated).
2. Soak cashews in a small basin of water.
3. After draining and rinsing the cashews, they should be flushed. Next, pour 1 cup of cold water into the blender with the cashews.
4. Blend till the cashews and water have a milk-like onsistency.

5. Add a handful of apple chunks to the mix. Blend until the liquid portion of the mixture is entirely gone. Continue to add the apple and banana in small handfuls, mixing well after each addition until all fruit chunks have been incorporated.

176. GREEK FRAPPE

TOTAL TIME 3 mins

INGREDIENTS

- 1 tsp instant coffee only instant coffee will work
- 1 tsp sugar, xylitol, or one sweetener of choice
- 1 cup of water room temperature
- splash of milk of choice optional

INSTRUCTIONS

1. Blitz the instant coffee, sugar/sweetener, and water in your Nutribullet for around 20 seconds, or until exceedingly frothy.
2. Pour your Frappe into a large glass and top with a splash of milk (do not attempt to add milk before blitzing).
3. That concludes our discussion. Take pleasure in it.

177. EASY GREEK FRAPPE RECIPE

PREP TIME 1 minute

TOTAL TIME 1 minute

Ingredients

- 2 Tsp Instant Coffee
- 1-2 Tsp Of Granulated Sugar
- 2 Tbsp Of Water
- Non-dairy Milk [Any kind works]
- Vegan Creamer [I use Silk brand]

- Ice, for serving

Instructions

1. Combine instant coffee, granulated sugar, and water in a jar. To aid foaming, add 2-3 ice cubes to the container.
2. Shake for 30 seconds or until a thick foam/froth has developed. The foam may be lesser if you use decaf coffee, but the ice will help froth it up!
3. Fill a glass halfway with ice, and then pour the coffee foam on top. Next, fill the remaining 1/3 of the glass with creamer and the remaining 2/3 with milk.
4. Serve immediately, swirling the flavors with a straw or spoon.!

178. DALGONA WHIPPED COFFEE VS THE GREEK FRAPPE

Ingredients

For the Dalgona Coffee:

- 1-2 servings:
- 2 tbsp of instant coffee
- 2 tbsp of granulated sugar
- 2 tbsp of cold water
- optional: splash of vanilla extract
- ice and milk or steamed milk
- optional toppings: cinnamon and cocoa powder
- For the Frappe (1 serving):
- Sweet: 1-2 tsp instant coffee + 4 tsp sugar
- medium: 1-2 tsp instant coffee + 2 tsp sugar
- plain: 1-2 tsp instant coffee and no sugar
- ice
- water
- milk (optional)

Instructions

1. For the Dalgona Coffee, follow these instructions:
2. In a mixing bowl, combine the coffee, sugar, water, and vanilla extract; beat on high speed with an electric mixer until thick and

glossy. Dollop the whipped coffee on top of hot or cold milk in a glass. Serve with a cinnamon and cocoa powder garnish.
3. To make the Frappe:
4. In a shaker, combine the coffee, sugar, and 2-3 tablespoons cold water and rapidly mix until thick froth forms. Alternatively, use a milk frother or a milkshake machine to combine the ingredients.
5. Fill a large glass halfway with ice cubes and pour the foam in. Fill with milk and water and serve right away.

179. HOW TO MAKE FRAPPE – GREEK ICED COFFEE

Prep Time 2 mins

Ingredients

- 2 tsp instant coffee
- ½ tsp sugar
- cold water
- cold milk
- ice cubes

Instructions

1. The amount of each component will vary depending on the size of the glass you use and, of course, your personal preferences. For example, I used a drink that was 16cm tall and 8cm broad.
2. Add the coffee, sugar, and a couple of inches of water. Use a frappe mixer or a milkshake to whip the mixture until it forms a thick, non-dripping foam. Then, depending on your preferences, add the ice cubes, ice water, and a small amount of milk. Take pleasure in it!

180. DALTON COFFEE VS GREEK FRAPPE

Ingredients

- 2 tbsp. granulated sugar
- 2 tbsp. instant coffee
- 2 tbsp. cold water
- Ice, for serving
- Milk, for serving

Directions

1. Combine the sugar, coffee, and water in a medium mixing basin. Hand-whisk the mixture until it becomes silky smooth and shiny, then continue whisking until it thickens and retains its shape, about 3-5 minutes by hand and 1 minute with the whisk attachment in a stand mixer.
2. Fill a glass halfway with ice and milk, then top with the whipped coffee mixture, stir, and serve...

181. GREEK ICED COFFEE

Total: 15 mins

Ingredients

- 2 tsp instant coffee
- 1-2 tsp sugar
- Two ice cubes
- ¼ cup of cold water
- ⅓ cup of chilled milk

Direction

1. In a jar with a tight-fitting lid, combine instant coffee, sugar, ice cubes, and water; shake vigorously for 30 seconds or until frothy. Add the milk and mix well...

Nutrition Facts

Serving Size: 1/2 Cup of Per Serving: 57 calories; protein 3g; carbohydrates 9.8g; sugars 8.3g; fat 0.8g; saturated fat 0.5g; cholesterol 4.1mg; vitamin a iu 159.3IU; folate 4.1mcg; calcium 106.2mg; iron 0.1mg; magnesium 16.1mg; potassium 193.3mg; sodium 38.3mg

182. NESCAFE FRAPPE

Ingredients

- 1 tbsp. quality instant espresso powder
- 1/3 cup of cold water
- 4-5 ice cubes
- 4 tsp. sugar (or more)
- 1-2 tbsp. milk

Instructions

2. FILL A BLENDER HALFWAY WITH COLD WATER AND BLEND ON HIGH FOR 30 SECONDS, OR UNTIL FROTHY. POUR THE FOAMY ESPRESSO OVER ICE CUBES IN A LARGE 16-OUNCE GLASS. AS NEEDED, ADD THE SUGAR, THEN THE MILK, AND WHISK THOROUGHLY.

183. MATCHA FRAPPE

PREP TIME 10 mins

COOK TIME 1 min

INGREDIENTS

- 1 tsp high-quality matcha powder
- 5 oz. hot, not boiling, water 175-180 degrees
- 1 Tbsp sugar
- 2 oz whole milk
- 1 cup of ice

INSTRUCTIONS

3. In a tea kettle, bring water to a boil. Then, turn off the heat and wait a few minutes for the temperature to drop (matcha is best made with very hot but not boiling water).
4. Measure a tsp of matcha powder into a small bowl while the water cools gently. 5 oz boiling water, poured over matcha powder To blend, vigorously stir with a tiny whisk.
5. Add the sugar to the matcha and mix until it has been completely dissolved.
6. Pour in the milk. Tea should be refrigerated for 20 minutes.

184. NUTRIBULLET BEAUTY BLAST SMOOTHIE RECIPE

PREP TIME 4 minutes

COOK TIME 1 minute

TOTAL TIME 5 minutes

INGREDIENTS

- ½ cup of pineapple
- ½ cup of strawberries, frozen
- 2 cups of swiss chard
- 1 tbsp goji berries
- 12 cashew nuts
- ½ cup of water
- ½ cup of ice
- Collagen Boost (optional)

INSTRUCTIONS

1. Place ingredients into a blender, fill to the max water line and blend until a smooth consistency is achieved.

185. GRAPE JUICE FRESHLY MADE

Ingredients

- 1 pound seedless grapes
- 1/2 cup of water

Instructions

2. Remove the stems from the grapes and wash them.
3. Blend the grapes with the water in a blender.
4. Blend for at least 1 minute on high.
5. Strain the mixture through a fine-mesh sieve into a large mixing basin, pressing down with a large spoon to extract all of the juice.
6. Drink right away, then refrigerate the rest in sealed jars.
7. Enjoy your 'Freshly Made Grape Juice.'

186. ROASTED STRAWBERRY PROTEIN SMOOTHIE

REP TIME: 3 mins

COOK TIME: 12 mins

TOTAL TIME: 15 mins

INGREDIENTS

- 1-1/2 cups of fresh strawberries, quartered
- 1/2 tbsp raw sugar
- 1/3 cup of reduced-fat cottage cheese
- 1/2 cup of fat-free milk
- 1 cup of crushed ice
- 1 tsp chia seeds
- 6 to 8 drops liquid stevia, optional

INSTRUCTIONS

1. Preheat oven to 425°F.

187. IN A MEDIUM BOWL, CARROT ORANGE BANANA SMOOTHIES

Ingredients

- Five carrots roughly chopped
- Three oranges - peeled and removed of pith
- 4 cups of cold water
- Three very ripe bananas
- One heaping tbsp flaxseed
- splash of vanilla extract

Instructions

2. Add water, carrots, and oranges to a high-powered blender. Blend until smooth and well combined.
3. In a large mixing basin, strain the carrots and oranges, pushing on the particles to obtain as much juice as possible.

4. Add the bananas, flaxseed, and vanilla extract to the recently strained juice in the blender. Blend until completely smooth. 8 oz glasses should be used for serving.
5. Serves 6

188. DELICIOUS MUNG BEAN SPROUTS JUICE & SMOOTHIE RECIPE

Prep: 5 mins

Cook: 0 mins

Total: 5 mins

Ingredients

- Mung Mango Delight!
- 1 Mango (chunked without the seed or skin)
- A handful of fresh Mung Bean Sprouts
- 1/2 Cucumber (with the skin)
- 1 cup of Coconut (fresh chunked)
- for a smoothie, add 1-2 cups of Coconut water or milk

INSTRUCTIONS

1. I love this juice most of all for its sweet fresh, healthy flavor without any added sugar!

189. CREAMY CAULIFLOWER SOUP

PREP TIME: 5 mins

COOK TIME: 25 mins

TOTAL TIME: 30 mins

INGREDIENTS

- 1 tbsp butter
- 1 tbsp unbleveryed flour, gluten-free is fine too
- One medium head cauliflower, chopped
- 1/2 cup of chopped onions

- 4 cups of less-sodium chicken broth, vegetarians can use vegetable broth
- salt and pepper as need

INSTRUCTIONS

2. Melt the butter in a medium pot over low heat to produce a roux.
3. Stir in the flour for about 2 minutes.
4. Set the heat to medium and add the chicken broth, onions, and cauliflower.
5. Bring to a boil, then reduce to a low heat and continue to cook until the vegetables are soft (about 20 minutes.)
6. Using an immersion blender, puree until smooth. Salt & pepper to taste.

190. CREAMY CAULIFLOWER COMFORT SOUP

Ingredients

- 2 cup of cauliflower, chopped and steamed
- 2 cup of almond milk, unsweetened
- 1/4 tsp garlic powder
- 1/4 tsp sea salt
- 1/4 tsp black pepper, ground

Directions

1. Allow the steamed cauliflower to cool to room temperature before serving.
2. In your NutriBullet Rx Soup Pitcher, combine all ingredients and extract on the 7-Minute Heated Cycle
3. Have fun!
4. Alternatively, puree all of the thoroughly cooled ingredients in a blender until smooth, then transfer to a pot and simmer until warm.

Nutritional information

Calories: 66.5

Total Fat: 2.9 g   4.4%

Saturated Fat: 0.3 g   1.4%

Cholesterol: 0 mg   0%

Sodium: 486.6 mg   20.3%

Total Carbs: 8.7 g   2.9%

191. CREAMY CAULIFLOWER & POTATO SOUP

Prep Time 5 minutes

Cook Time 25 minutes

Total Time 30 minutes

INGREDIENTS

- 2 tbsp olive oil + more for garnish
- Two leeks dark leaves removed, quartered, sliced, and cleaned
- kosher salt as need
- Four russet potatoes peeled and cut into 2-inch chunks
- One small head of cauliflower florets removed
- 5 cups of vegetable stock
- freshly ground pepper as need

INSTRUCTIONS

1. Heat olive oil in a Dutch oven or large saucepan over medium-low heat. Season with salt and simmer; they occasionally stir until the leeks are wilted and translucent, about 5 to 7 minutes. 1/4 cup of the leeks should be set aside for garnish, and the remainder should be left in the saucepan.
2. Combine the potatoes, cauliflower, and vegetable stock in a large mixing bowl. Bring to a boil, then reduce to low heat. Cook until the potatoes are soft when pierced with a fork.
3. In a blender, purée the soup in small batches. Return the soup to the stove and season with salt and pepper as needed. If you have an immersion blender, this will be much easier. If the soup is too thick, add a little more stock.
4. If wanted, serve the soup hot, garnished with the reserved leeks and a sprinkle of olive oil.

NUTRITION

Calories: 205kcal | Carbohydrates: 37g | Protein: 5g | Fat: 5g | Saturated Fat: 1g | Sodium: 825mg | Potassium: 932mg | Fiber: 4g | Sugar: 6g | Vitamin A: 912IU | Vitamin C: 58mg | Calcium: 57mg | Iron: 2mg

192. CREAMY CAULIFLOWER WILD RICE SOUP

PREP TIME: 10 MINS

COOK TIME: 45 MINS

TOTAL TIME: 55 MINUTES

INGREDIENTS

- 1 cup of chopped celery (150 g)
- One medium white onion, diced (approx. 1 1/2 cups of 215 g)
- Threeminced cloves garlic,
- 1 tsp every ground thyme and oregano
- 2 cups of peeled and diced carrots (300 g)
- Four heaping cups of or one small head of cauliflower, chopped into small florets (450 g)
- 5 cups of vegetable broth
- 1/2 cup of nutritional yeast (30 g)
- 1 1/2 cups of cooked wild rice (250 g)
- 1 tsp every sea salt and black pepper, or more as need
- a squeeze of fresh lemon juice (1-2 tbsp)

INSTRUCTIONS

1. Cook the wild rice as directed on the packet. Continue to make the soup while it's simmering.
2. COOK THE ONION, GARLIC, AND CELERY IN A 7.5 QT SOUP POT WITH 2 TBSP WATER FOR ABOUT 5 MINUTES, OR UNTIL THEY BEGIN TO SOFTEN, STIRRING FREQUENTLY (ALTERNATIVELY, YOU CAN SAUTE THE VEGGIES IN 1 TBSP OF OLIVE OIL). ADD ADDITIONAL TBSP OF WATER IF THE POT BEGINS TO DRY OUT AT

ANY POINT. COOK FOR ANOTHER 2 MINUTES, STIRRING CONSTANTLY UNTIL THE THYME AND OREGANO ARE AROMATIC.
3. Simmer the cauliflower, carrots, and all of the vegetable stock until the carrots and cauliflower are soft, about 15 minutes. This should take about 20 minutes to complete.

4. Add the nutritional yeast and mix well.
5. Half of the soup should be blended. Make sure the lid has a crack in it to allow the steam to escape. Begin blending on low and then increase to high until the mixture is smooth and creamy. Pour it back into the soup pot with the remainder of the soup once it's been blended.

193. IMMUNITY BLAST SMOOTHIE

PREP TIME5 minutes

COOK TIME5 minutes

TOTAL TIME10 minutes

INGREDIENTS

- 1 cup of spinach
- Four medium strawberries
- 1/3 cup of pineapple chunks
- One medium peeled kiwi
- Ten almonds
- Eight fl0unces orange juice
- Four ice cubes

INSTRUCTIONS

1. Combine all of the ingredients in a blender.
2. Blend everything until it's smooth and uniform.
3. Add more ice cubes for a thicker consistency.

4. Serve right away.

Nutrition Information:

Amount Per Serving: CALORIES: 317TOTAL FAT: 7gSATURATED FAT: 0.5gTRANS FAT: 0gCHOLESTEROL: 0mgSODIUM: 556mgCARBOHYDRATES: 59gFIBER: 1 1gSUGAR: 39gPROTEIN: 11g

194. FRESH LEMON GINGER DETOXIFYING SMOOTHIE

prep time: 5 MINUTES

total time: 5 MINUTES

Ingredients

- 1/2 cup of frozen every
- 1/2 cup of frozen pineapple
- 1/2 cup of frozen mango
- juice of 1 whole, large lemon
- 1/2 tbsp lemon zest
- 3/4 cup of unsweetened coconut milk (carton, not canned)
- 1 tbsp freshly grated ginger
- 1/2 tbsp raw honey
- 2 tbsp collagen peptides
- 1 tbsp chia seeds (optional)

Instructions

1. Combine all of the ingredients in a blender.
2. Blend everything until it's smooth and uniform.
3. Add more ice cubes for a thicker consistency.

195. BERRY BLAST SMOOTHIES

Prep Time 10 minutes

Total Time 10 minutes

Ingredients

- 3 cups of mixed frozen berries raspberries, blueberries, blackberries, thawed slightly
- 1 cup of fresh or frozen strawberries sliced (if using frozen thaw slightly first)
- 1 cup of light vanilla yogurt
- 1 Tbsp sugar
- 1 tsp vanilla extract
- 1 1/2 cups of orange juice

Instructions

1. Add all of the ingredients to a blender. Close with lid and blend until well mixed. Pour into glasses and enjoy!
2. (If you like a thicker smoothie, just use less juice.)

Notes

Yields: about five one-cup of servings.

196.BERRY CRUNCH SMOOTHIE BOWL

INGREDIENTS

smoothie bowl:

Two small frozen bananas

One packet of pitaya + dragon fruit

1/3 cup of unsweetened vanilla almond milk

toppings:

vanilla granola

goji berries

unsweetened coconut flakes

INSTRUCTIONS

1. Add smoothie bowl ingredients to nutribullet and blend until "ice cream" consistency.

2. Pour into bowl of choice and add toppings.

196.BERRY DRAGON FRUIT SMOOTHIE

INGREDIENTS

Smoothie:

- 1 cup of frozen raspberries
- One ¾ cups of frozen pink dragon fruit (200 grams)
- ½ cup of frozen blackberries
- 5.3 ounces strawberry Greek yogurt (150 grams)
- 2 tbsp chia seeds
- 1 tsp lime juice (½ lime)
- 1 tsp grated ginger
- 1 cup of unsweetened almond milk

INSTRUCTIONS

1. In a blender container, combine raspberries, dragon fruit, blackberries, yogurt, chia seeds, lime, and ginger. Cover and blend on high until smooth, adding almond milk as needed. If necessary, scrape the sides of the container with a spatula. If the smoothie is too thick, add more almond milk until it reaches the required consistency.
2. If preferred, pour the smoothie into a glass and top with more chia seeds and berries...

NUTRITION

Serving: 62.5g | Calories: 284kcal | Carbohydrates: 43g | Protein: 11.2g | Fat: 8.3g | Saturated Fat: 1.8g | Polyunsaturated Fat: 3.6g | Monounsaturated Fat: 1.8g | Cholesterol: 9.8mg | Sodium: 122mg | Potassium: 11.2mg | Fiber: 14.7g | Sugar: 23.3g | Vitamin A: 202.6IU | Vitamin C: 20.5mg | Calcium: 713mg | Iron: 2.5mg

197.PERFECT DRAGON FRUIT SMOOTHIE

Prep Time: 5 minutes

Ingredients

- 7 ounces frozen dragonfruit puree (two 3.5 ounce packets)
- ½ cup of cold water
- 1 cup of frozen pineapple chunks
- ½ cup of frozen diced or fresh mango
- One large banana (room temperature)
- 1 tbsp lime juice (optional)
- Optional: See protein adders above!

Instructions

1. Remove the package of the dragonfruit puree and thaw it in warm water so it can be split into smaller chunks, then add the pieces to the mixer. Pour in the water, then add the pineapple, mango, and banana chunks.
2. Blend until smooth, stop and scrap as needed, and add a little more cold water if necessary to make a puree (you'll need more water with frozen mango vs. fresh mango).
3. If desired, add the lime juice after tasting. Serve right away, or store in an airtight jar for up to 1 day.

198. CREAMY DRAGON FRUIT SMOOTHIE BOWL

PREP TIME 5 minutes

TOTAL TIME 5 minutes

Ingredients

- 2 packets frozen dragon fruit* (unsweetened // we like Pitaya+ brand)
- 1/2 cup of frozen raspberries (or other fruit of choice)
- Two medium ripe bananas previously peeled, sliced, and frozen
- 3 Tbsp Vegan Vanilla Protein Powder (right now, we like Nuzest and Tropeaka)

- 1/4 - 1/2 cup of dairy-free milk (we used DIY Coconut Milk)
- TOPPINGS optional
- Coconut flakes
- Fresh fruit
- Hemp seeds
- Granola

Instructions

1. Frozen dragon fruit, frozen raspberries, banana, protein powder, and dairy-free milk in a high-powered blender (starting with the lower end of the range). Blend until the mixture is creamy and smooth. The key to making a thick smoothie bowl is to be patient and blend slowly, adding only as much liquid as needed and scraping the sides down with a smoothie wand (or something similar that's blender friendly) while it combines.
2. Taste and adjust the seasonings as needed, adding an extra banana for sweetness, dairy-free milk for smoothness, or berries for a more spicy berry taste.
3. Divide amongst serving bowls and top with fruit, granola, hemp seeds, and coconut flakes if desired (optional).
4. When it's fresh, it's the best. Leftovers can be kept in the refrigerator for up to 24 hours. Then, freeze to store for a more extended period. Alternatively, freeze in an ice cube shape for future smoothies.

Nutrition

Calories: 225

Carbohydrates: 48 g

Protein: 8.1 g

Fat: 1.6 g

Saturated Fat: 0.6 g

Polyunsaturated Fat: 0.11 g

Monounsaturated Fat: 0.08 g

Trans Fat: 0 g

Cholesterol: 0 mg

Sodium: 92 mg

Potassium: 552 mg

199. DRAGON FRUIT (PITAYA) SMOOTHIE BOWL

Prep Time: 5 minutes

Total Time: 5 minutes

Ingredients

Smoothie Bowl:

- 6 ounces frozen pitaya (dragon fruit)
- 1/2 cup of unsweetened almond milk
- 1/2 banana (preferably frozen)
- 1 cup of pineapple chunks (preferably frozen)
- 1 cup of mango chunks (preferably frozen)
- Optional Toppings:
- Blueberries
- Raspberries
- Strawberries
- Kiwi
- Goji berries
- Bee Pollen
- Cacao Nibs
- Coconut
- Pumpkin Seeds
- Almonds
- Chia seeds

Instructions

1. Place smoothie bowl ingredients in blender and process until smooth.
2. Add toppings to your heart's desire – Time to get creative!

200. PINK PITAYA PROTEIN SMOOTHIE

Total Time: 5 minutes

INGREDIENTS

- One frozen ripe banana
- 1 serving fresh or frozen pitaya (pink dragonfruit)
- 1/2 cup of frozen raspberries
- 2 tbsp vanilla vegan yogurt
- plant milk to blend
- optional
- 1/2 cup of frozen mango
- 1 serving vanilla plant protein powder

INSTRUCTIONS

1. In a high-powered blender, combine all ingredients, starting with less plant milk and adding more as needed to mix. Use a small amount of plant milk for a thicker smoothie bowl texture and more for a drinkable smoothie.

201. DRAGON FRUIT AND YOGURT SMOOTHIE RECIPE

Prep Time: 05 mins

Cook Time: 15 mins

Ingredients

- Of Dragon Fruit And Yogurt Smoothie
- 1 Dragon fruit
- 2 Fresh apricots
- 2 drops Sugar substitute
- 2 tbsp Hung yogurt
- 1/2 cup of Milk
- 3 tbsp Corn cereal

Instructions

2. Peel and cut the dragon fruit into chunks.

3. Deseed and dice up the apricots and put them in a blender along with the dragon fruit.
4. Put the sugar drops, yogurt, and milk and give it a nice blend.
5. Add some ice cubes to cool it quickly.
6. Add the corn flakes.

202. DRAGON FRUIT MANGO SMOOTHIE

prep time: 5 MINUTES

cook time: 5 MINUTES

total time: 10 MINUTES

Ingredients

- 1 Dragon fruit, cubed
- One mango cubed/chopped
- 4-6 ice cubes
- 3 tbsp raw cane sugar or honey
- 1 tsp vanilla
- 1 cup of almond milk
- 1/2 a scoop vanilla protein powder of your choice, optional

Instructions

7. Place ALL the ingredients in a blender and blend till smooth - this smoothie will be thick - we gulped ours down sans straws.

203. DRAGON FRUIT BLACKBERRY SMOOTHIE

prep time: 2 MINUTES

total time: 2 MINUTES

Ingredients

- 1/2 of 1 Dragon Fruit
- 1/2 cup of blackberries
- Two leaves kale washed and chopped
- 1 tbsp ground flax
- 1/2 cup of milk
- ice

Instructions

1. Cut the Dragon Fruit in half and remove the fruit from the peel with a spoon.
2. 2Combine the kale, flax, and blackberries in a blender or smoothie maker.
3. The Dragon Fruit, ice, and milk are then added.
4. Blend until completely smooth.
5. Pour into your favorite glass and enjoy

204.DRAGON FRUIT CHIA COCONUT PUDDING SMOOTHIE

prep time: 5 MINUTES

additional time: 15 MINUTES

total time: 20 MINUTES

Ingredients

- One large banana, peeled, quartered, frozen
- 1 ½ cups of pitaya, cubed, frozen
- ¾ cups of plant-based milk
- 1 tbsp almond butter
- 1 tsp agave
- 1 tbsp chia seeds

Instructions

1. A version in a hurry
2. Blend frozen fruits, plant-based milk, almond butter, agave, and chia seeds until extremely smooth in a high-powered blender.
3. Taste and make any necessary adjustments to the flavor. Add more agave if you want it sweeter or more almond milk if you want it thinner.
4. Serve immediately in a large glass or two medium drinks.
5. Version with more pauses

Nutrition Information

Amount Per Serving: CALORIES: 246TOTAL FAT: 9gSATURATED FAT: 2gTRANS FAT: 0gUNSATURATED FAT: 6gCHOLESTEROL: 7mgSODIUM: 56mgCARBOHYDRATES: 39gFIBER: 7gSUGAR: 18gPROTEIN: 8g

205. RASPBERRY COCONUT DRAGON FRUIT SMOOTHIE BOWLS

Prep Time 15 mins

Total Time 15 mins

Ingredients

- One dragon fruit peeled & sliced
- 1/2 cup of raspberries
- Three bananas peeled & sliced
- 30 ml coconut milk

Instructions

1. In a blender, combine all ingredients and process about eight times until smooth.
2. Fill two bowls with the mixture and top with fresh fruit.
3. Smoothie with tropical dragon fruit

206. DRAGON FRUIT AND A PINCH OF HONEY.

INGREDIENTS

- 1/2 cup of water
- 1 cup of pineapple (diced and frozen)
- 1 cup of mango (chopped and frozen)
- 1 cup of dragon fruit (chopped and frozen)
- 1 cup of strawberries (hulled and frozen)
- One banana
- honey

INSTRUCTIONS

1. Pineapple, mango, strawberries, and dragon fruit should all be washed and diced. Place in the freezer for at least 2 hours.
2. Blend the frozen fruit with one peeled banana and a splash of honey in a blender. Blend until completely smooth.

3. Two glasses to serve.

207. DAIRY-FREE DRAGONFRUIT SMOOTHIE BOWL

PREP TIME 5 mins

TOTAL TIME 5 mins

Ingredients

- 7 frozen dragon fruit puree with or without seeds (whichever you prefer)
- 1/2 cup of frozen cherries pitted
- 1/2 banana
- 1/2 cup of frozen passion fruit
- 4 orange juice or more for a thinner consistency
- Chopped fresh fruit for garnish (optional)

Instructions

1. Fill a high-powered blender halfway with orange juice, then add the remaining ingredients.
2. Blend on high until you have the desired consistency. If the smoothie is too thick, add a splash of orange juice at a time. *
3. Fill a bowl halfway with your smoothie and top with fresh fruit and edible flowers, if desired.

Nutrition

Calories: 381kcal | Carbohydrates: 82g | Protein: 5g | Fat: 4g | Saturated Fat: 1g | Sodium: 154mg | Potassium: 1002mg | Fiber: 17g | Sugar: 55g | Vitamin A: 1810IU | Vitamin C: 102mg | Calcium: 39mg | Iron: 5mg

208. ALMOND BANANA DRAGON FRUIT BOWL

INGREDIENTS

- 1 Pitaya + Smoothie pack
- One frozen banana

- 1/4 cup of frozen mango
- 1/2 Tbsp crunchy almond butter
- 1/2 cup of unsweetened vanilla almond milk
- Toppings: banana slices, toasted almonds, homemade granola

INSTRUCTIONS

1. In a blender, combine all of the ingredients. Blend until smooth, adding more almond milk as needed to achieve the desired consistency.

NUTRITION

Serving: 1bowl without toppings

Calories: 269kcal

Carbohydrates: 57g

Protein: 6g

Fat: 12g

Fiber: 10g

Sugar: 36g

209. HEALTHY DRAGON FRUIT SMOOTHIE

Prep Time: 3 minutes

Cook Time: 2 minutes

Total Time: 5 minutes

Ingredients

- 2 cups of dragon fruit, two frozen pitaya packs, or one medium dragon fruit*
- 1/2 cup of almond milk** unsweetened
- One giant whole banana*** frozen
- Toppings (Optional)
- granola and seeds such as chia seeds
- fresh fruits such as kiwi, banana, blueberries, strawberries

Instructions

2. If using fresh dragon fruit, cut it into little cubes and place it in the freezer overnight. (You can use frozen pitaya packs straight from the freezer.)
3. Combine all of the ingredients and cut the frozen banana into bits.
4. To begin, pour the almond milk into the blender.
5. Combine the frozen banana and dragon fruit in a bowl.
6. Secure the lid and begin blending on low, gradually increasing to high. Blend for 30 to 60 seconds, or until the mixture is smooth and uniformly distributed. (Add more almond milk if the smoothie is too thick; if it's too thin, add additional fruits.)

210. TRIPLE CHERRY BERRY WATERMELON SMOOTHIE

PREP TIME 5 MINS

COOK TIME 0 MINS

TOTAL TIME 5 MINS

Ingredients

- One large frozen banana
- 1/2 cup of frozen strawberries
- 1/2 cup of frozen raspberries
- 1/2 cup of frozen cherries
- 1 cup of fresh cubed watermelon
- 1/2 cup of unsweetened almond milk

Instructions

1. Blend all of the ingredients in a blender. If required, add extra almond milk to assist combine the ingredients until they are smooth. It makes two smoothies.

Nutrition

Servings: 2 smoothies

Serving size: 1 smoothie

Calories: 137kcal

Fat: 1.2g

Carbohydrates: 32.6g

Fiber: 6g

Sugar: 19.9g

Protein: 2.3g

211. BLUEBERRY WATERMELON SMOOTHIE RECIPE

Prep Time 2 mins

Total Time 2 mins

Ingredients

- 3 cups of blueberries
- 3 cups of cubed watermelon
- 1 1/2 cups of ice

Instructions

2. In a blender container, combine blueberries and watermelon. Blend for about 40 seconds on high or until the mixture is thoroughly pureed. Then turn off the mixer and take off the lid. Replace the cover on the container and add ice to the puree. Blend for another 40 seconds on high, or until the mixture is perfectly smooth and there are no ice chunks left.
3. Serve immediately.

Nutrition Information

Calories: 65kcal | Carbohydrates: 16g | Protein: 1g | Fat: 1g | Saturated Fat: 1g | Sodium: 2mg | Potassium: 142mg | Fiber: 2g | Sugar: 12g | Vitamin A: 470IU | Vitamin C: 13.4mg | Calcium: 10mg | Iron: 0.4mg

212. WATERMELON RASPBERRY SMOOTHIE

Prep Time 5 mins

Ingredients

- 500 g watermelon flesh
- 100 g raspberries
- 150 g Greek yogurt
- 3-4 ice cubes
- One tbs honey (optional)

Instructions

1. Cut the watermelon into bite-size chunks with a knife.
2. BLEND THE MELON, RASPBERRIES, GREEK YOGURT, AND ICE CUBES IN A BLENDER.
3. Blend in as much honey as needed until smooth. Serve right away.

213. PALEO WATERMELON BERRY SMOOTHIE

Prep Time: 5 mins

Total Time: 5 mins

Ingredients

- 2 cups of cubed watermelon
- 1 cup of fresh raspberries
- 1 cup of frozen blueberries
- 1 cup of ice

Instructions

1. Add all ingredients to a high-speed blender in the order listed and blend until smooth.

Nutrition

Calories: 59kcal Carbohydrates: 15g Protein: 1g Fat: 1g Saturated Fat: 1g Sodium: 2mg Potassium: 159mg Fiber: 3g Sugar: 10g Vitamin A: 455IU Vitamin C: 17.6mg Calcium: 13mg Iron: 0.5mg

214. VEGAN + GF

INGREDIENTS

- 1/2 cup of water (125 ml)*
- 2 cup of fresh watermelon, cubed (300g)**
- 1/3 cup of tofu (80g)***
- 1 cup of mixed frozen berries (125g)
- One small banana, frozen (120g)
- pinch of salt

INSTRUCTIONS

2. Add all the ingredients into a blender in the order listed. Blend until smooth & creamy!

NUTRITION

Serving Size: 1 Serving Calories: 318g Sugar: 44.5g Sodium: 173mg Fat: 3.6g Saturated Fat: 0.2g Unsaturated Fat: 0.4g Trans Fat: 0 Carbohydrates: 67.4g Fiber: 7.3g Protein: 10.6g Cholesterol: 0

215. CLEAN EATING TRIPLE BERRY WATERMELON SMOOTHIE

Prep Time: 10 minutes

Total Time: 10 minutes

Ingredients

- 2 cups of triple berry blend
- 2 cups of apple juice (no sugar added - 100% juice)
- 1 cup of fresh watermelon
- 1 tbsp. lemon juice

Instructions

3. Blend all ingredients in a blender until smooth and serve.

Notes

Please note that the nutrition data given here is a ballpark figure. Accurate data is not possible.

Nutrition

Serving: 1cup
of | Calories: 87kcal | Carbohydrates: 21g | Sodium: 4mg | Potassium: 167mg | Fiber: 1g | Sugar: 16g | Vitamin A: 200IU | Vitamin C: 6mg | Calcium: 15mg | Iron: 0.3mg

216. STRAWBERRY WATERMELON SMOOTHIE

Prep Time 5 mins

Cook Time 0 mins

Total Time 5 mins

Ingredients

- 4 cups of watermelon, diced, seedless
- 4 cups of strawberries, frozen
- 2 tbsp lime juice
- Six large mint leaves, fresh
- 2 tsp agave nectar, honey

Instructions

1. Add all ingredients into a blender.
2. Blend until smooth, about 30 seconds to 1 minute.
3. Equipment
4. Countertop Blender
5. Decorative Paper Straws

Nutrition Facts

Strawberry Watermelon Smoothie

Amount Per Serving

Calories 115 Calories from Fat 9

% Daily Value*

Fat 1g 2%

Saturated Fat 0.05g 0%

Polyunsaturated Fat 0.3g

Monounsaturated Fat 0.1g

Sodium 6mg0%

Potassium 406mg12%

Carbohydrates 28g9%

Fiber 4g16%

217. WATERMELON BERRY KALE SMOOTHIE

Prep Time 5 mins

Total Time 5 mins

Ingredients

- 2 cups of watermelon frozen and diced
- ¼ cup of coconut water
- 1 cup of kale stem removed and chopped
- ½ cup of frozen berry mix

Instructions

1. In a blender, combine the frozen watermelon, coconut water, kale, and mixed berries and process until everything is finely diced and the smoothie's consistency.

218. WATERMELON RASPBERRY MINT SMOOTHIE

PREP TIME: 5min

COOK TIME: 0min

Ingredients

- 2 cups of frozen and chopped watermelon
- 2 cups of almond milk
- 1/2 cup of frozen raspberries
- 1 tbsp lime juice
- 1 tbsp almond butter
- 1 tbsp maple syrup (or honey)

- Ten fresh mint leaves

Directions

1. In a high-powered blender, combine watermelon, almond milk, raspberries, lime juice, almond butter, maple syrup, and mint leaves until thick and smooth. Alternatively, combine the ingredients in a large mixing basin or saucepan and blend until smooth with an immersion blender.

220. MELON-BERRY MILKSHAKE

PREP TIME5 minutes

COOK TIME5 minutes

TOTAL TIME10 minutes

INGREDIENTS

- Two wedges of fresh cantaloupe, cut into chunks (about ¼ large melon)
- 1 cup of fresh or frozen blueberries
- 1 tbsp chia seeds
- About ½ cup of unsweetened plain almond milk (to fill line)
- Get IngredientsPowered by Chicory

INSTRUCTIONS

2. Place everything into the NutriBullet and blend until smooth. Makes two servings.

Nutrition Information:

Amount Per Serving: CALORIES: 117TOTAL FAT: 3.5gCHOLESTEROL: 0mgSODIUM: 81mgFIBER: 5.6gSUGAR: 15.6gPROTEIN: 3.3g

221. REFRESHING SUMMER SMOOTHIE RECIPE

Prep Time 5 minutes

Cook Time 0 minutes

Total Time 5 minutes

Ingredients

- 4 cups of watermelon chopped
- 1/2 avocado
- 6-8 ice cubes
- 1/4 cup of coconut water
- 1/2 cup of strawberries
- 2/3 mint leaves

Instructions

3. Make sure your watermelon is seed-free by prepping and chopping it.
4. To make it easy on the machine, all of the blender ingredients, starting with the watermelon.
5. Combine all ingredients in a blender and blend until smooth.

Nutrition Facts

Refreshing Summer Smoothie Recipe

Amount Per Serving

Calories 95Calories from Fat 36

% Daily Value*

222. TRIPLE BERRY BANANA SMOOTHIE RECIPE

prep time5 MINUTES

total time5 MINUTES

INGREDIENTS

- 1/2 banana
- 1 cup of fresh or frozen berries (raspberries, blueberries, blackberries)
- One scoop protein powder
- 1/3 cup of plant-based milk
- 2-3 ice cubes

INSTRUCTIONS

1. Add bananas, berries, protein powder, plant-based milk, and ice cubes to a blender or food processor.
2. Blend until smooth, then add more plant-based milk until the desired consistency is achieved.
3. Pour into a glass or bowl, garnish with more berries, and serve!

223. PEANUT BUTTER BLUEBERRY BANANA SMOOTHIE

Prep Time: 5 minutes

Total Time: 5 minutes

Ingredients

- 1/2 cup of frozen wild blueberries
- One small frozen banana
- 1 cup of fresh baby spinach
- 2 Tbsp. hemp seeds
- 1 Tbsp. salted peanut butter
- One scoop plant-based vanilla protein powder (sub collagen powder)
- 3/4 to 1 cup of Silk Vanilla Oatmilk

Instructions

1. In a high-powered blender, combine all ingredients and blend on the lowest setting. Increase to one-third power for 20 seconds before gradually increasing to the total capacity. Blend on high until the mixture is perfectly smooth and creamy.

Nutrition

Serving: 1smoothie | Calories: 470kcal | Carbohydrates: 45g | Protein: 27g | Fat: 22g | Saturated Fat: 2g | Sodium: 145mg | Fiber: 9g | Sugar: 20g

224. PEANUT BUTTER BLUEBERRY BANANA SMOOTHIE

PREP TIME5 MINUTES

TOTAL TIME5 MINUTES

Ingredients

For the smoothie:

- One ripe medium banana (frozen if you prefer)
- 1 cup of frozen blueberries
- 1 tbsp peanut butter (or any nut butter you'd like)
- 1 cup of unsweetened almond milk, + more to thin if necessary
- For toppings:
- Your favorite granola
- Drizzle of peanut butter
- Extra banana slices + blueberries

Instructions

2. In a blender, combine all of the ingredients and blend until smooth. Add oats, peanut butter, and extra frozen or fresh blueberries and banana slices to the top. One person To serve two people, double the recipe.

Nutrition Facts

Serving Size: 1 Cup of Per Serving: 139 calories; protein 4.4g; carbohydrates 28g; dietary fiber 4.3g; sugars 17.4g; fat 2g; saturated fat 0.1g; vitamin a in 264.5IU; vitamin c 66.3mg; folate 50.5mcg; calcium 25.1mg; iron 0.7mg; magnesium 31.3mg; potassium 421.4mg; sodium 18.6mg; thiamin 0.1mg. Exchanges:

2 Fruit, 1/2 Low-Fat Milk

226.NO BANANA BERRY SMOOTHIE BOWL (VEGAN)

Prep Time5 mins

Total Time5 mins

Ingredients

- 1¼ cups of frozen mixed berries (I like to use a mix of raspberries, strawberries & blackberries)
- ½ heaped cup of frozen riced cauliflower
- One large kale leaf
- Two Medjool dates

- 3 tbsp hemp seeds
- One scoop of your favorite protein powder

Instructions

3. In a blender, combine all of the ingredients with 1 cup of water.
4. Blend for 30 seconds on high and pour into a bowl.
5. Add berries, shredded coconut, and cacao nibs to the top. Take pleasure in it!

227. MUST-TRY FRUIT SMOOTHIE WITH SILKEN TOFU AND PEANUT BUTTER

Prep Time: 5 minutes

Cook Time: 0 minutes

Total Time: 5 minutes

Ingredients

- One box (1 box) silken tofu, about 1 lb/450 g, use two boxes if buying smaller aseptic silken tofu packages
- 1 cup of (140 g) cherries, frozen works well because they're pitted, thawed if possible
- 1 cup of (150 g) blueberries, frozen is often more cost-effective, softened if possible
- 1 tbsp (15 g) pineapples, frozen chunks for convenience, but you can also use fresh
- 1 tbsp (15 g) peanut butter, salted (or add a pinch of salt), skip or replace with another nut butter if desired

Instructions

1. To prepare the silken tofu, cut it into cubes.
2. In a blender, combine the silken tofu and the water.
3. In a blender, combine the frozen fruits and peanut butter.
4. To make a smoothie, combine the silken tofu, fruits, and peanut butter in a blender. To get a uniform mix, you may need to pause the blender and stir the smoothie or push down the fruits that cling to the sides of the blender.

228. SPINACH BLUEBERRY AND BANANA SMOOTHIE

INGREDIENTS

2 cups of baby spinach, washed and rinsed

Two ripe bananas, peeled

2 cups of almond milk, unsweetened

½ cup of blueberries, fresh

½ cup of wheat germ or bran

2 tbsp ground flaxseed

2 tbsp almond butter

2 tsp pure vanilla extract

Two handfuls, ice cubes

DIRECTIONS

1. Fill your blender's canister halfway with ice. Combine the remaining ingredients and stir well.
2. Secure the cover on the blender and process until the smoothie is smooth.
3. Pour into elegant drinking glasses and enjoy right now!

229. BLUEBERRY CHEESECAKE SMOOTHIE

Prep Time: 5 minutes

Cook Time: 5 minutes

Total Time: 10 minutes

- 1 cup of frozen mixed berries
- One frozen ripe banana
- 1/2 cup of low-fat vanilla yogurt
- 1/4 cup of orange juice
- 1 tsp honey (optional)

Directions

Mix all ingredients in a blender and puree until smooth

231. VEGA BLUEBERRY VANILLA SMOOTHIE

5minPrep

5minTotal

Ingredients

- One scoop(s) Vanilla Vega Protein & Greens powder
- 1 ½ cup . Hy-Vee unsweetened vanilla almond milk
- ½ c. fresh spinach, optional
- One cup . Hy-Vee frozen blueberries
- ½ ripe banana
- ½ cup . ice
- One splash of fresh lemon juice

Directions

1. Add vanilla Vega, almond milk, spinach, frozen blueberries, banana, ice, and lemon juice in a blender. Blend until smooth.

Nutrition facts

Servings

280 Calories per Serving

232. CHOCOLATE BANANA PROTEIN SMOOTHIE

PREP TIME: 10 MINS

COOK TIME: 0 MINS

TOTAL TIME: 10 MINS

Ingredients

- 1.5 cups of O Organics plain unsweetened almond milk

- One large banana, frozen and cut into chunks
- One scoop Open Nature chocolate plant-based protein powder
- 2 tbsp Open Nature creamy maple almond butter
- 1.5 tbsp unsweetened cocoa powder

Instructions

2. Place all ingredients in a blender in the order listed and blend until smooth.
3. Pour into glasses and enjoy immediately.

233. DAIRY-FREE MANGO COLADA SMOOTHIES OR SMOOTHIE BOWLS

Prep time 5 mins

Ingredients

- 8 ounces (about 1-1/2 cups of) cubed frozen mango
- ½ cup of canned pineapple with juice
- ½ cup of canned coconut milk (total fat)
- ½ cup of to 1 cup of lite coconut milk
- 2 tbsp shredded unsweetened coconut (optional, but adds to the flavor and texture)

Instructions

1. In a blender, combine the mango, pineapple with juice, coconut milk, 12 cup lite coconut milk or milk beverage, and coconut (if using). Blend until the mixture is smooth and creamy. If it's too thick, add more lite coconut milk or milk beverage to thin it out.
2. Serve immediately by dividing the smoothie between two glasses, or see the Smoothie Bowl Option below.

Nutrition Information

Serving size: ½ batch Calories: 245 Fat: 15g Carbohydrates: 31g Sugar: 26g (0g added)

234. MANGO BASIL COLADA RECIPE

Prep Time: 05 mins

Cook Time: 05 mins

Total Cook Time: 10 mins

Ingredients

- Of Mango Basil Colada
- 100 gms fresh-cut mangoes
- 100 ml coconut water
- 50 ml coconut cream
- Ice
- 3 Basil leaves
- 1 tsp sugar
- How to Make Mango Basil Colada
- 1.Muddle the basil leaves in a glass with sugar.
- 2.Add ice, mangoes, and coconut water in a blender and mix.
- 3.Pour it in the basil glass.
- 4.While swirling it's with a spoon, add the fresh coconut cream.
- 5.Dress with the basil leaf

235.MANGO PIÑA COLADA COCKTAIL

Prep Time: 5 minutes

Total Time: 5 minutes

INGREDIENTS

- 6 oz white rum
- 4 oz dark rum
- 6 Ounces cream of coconut
- 4 Ounces pineapple juice
- 1 Ounces fresh lime juice
- 1 cup of frozen pineapple cubes
- 1 cup of frozen mango cubes
- 2-3 cups of ice

INSTRUCTIONS

1. In a high-powered blender, combine the frozen fruit, rum, pineapple juice, and coconut cream.
2. While the machine is running, add handfuls of ice until the drink has a slushy, thicker smoothie consistency.
3. Pour the colada into serving glasses, decorate with fresh fruit, and do right away.

236. SKINNY MANGO COLADA WITH (OPTIONAL) JALAPEÑOS

Prep Time 6 mins

Total Time 6 mins

Ingredients

- Mango puree
- 1 cup of chopped ripe mangoes
- 1/4 cup of water
- 2-5 tablespoons sugar, depending on the sweetness of mangoes
- Mango Colada
- 1/2 cup of coconut water, I used Harmless harvest
- 1/4 cup of mango puree
- 1/4 cup of white rum
- To serve,
- jalapeños ice cubes, optional

Instructions

1. Making Mango Puree
2. Chop the mangoes and combine them with the water and sugar in a mini mixer. Blend until completely smooth (can be made up to days ahead and stored in the refrigerator).
3. To prepare a mango colada, combine all of the ingredients in a blender and blend.
4. Combine ice cubes, coconut water, mango puree, and rum in a cocktail shaker. Shake vigorously and strain into a glass with ice (jalapenos or regular).

237. MANGO COLADA WITH BANANA AND GRAPEFRUIT

INGREDIENTS

- One smaller banana
- 2 ounces of rum- either all light or half light and half dark
- 4 ounces mango juice- I used the trader joe's brand, which is unsweetened and not from concentrate
- 2 ounces coconut cream I buy the small tetra packs from the Asian market rather than the sweetened stuff in the mixer section of your neighborhood market
- 1-ounce fresh grapefruit juice approximately

INSTRUCTIONS

1. Freeze the ingredients ahead of time if possible. I combine the rum, coconut, and mango for however many cocktails I'll be preparing, then freeze it with a few ripe, unpeeled bananas. If your bananas are enormous, you may only need half a banana. Combine all of the ingredients in a blender and blend until smooth. Garnish with a grapefruit slice.

238. CARNIVAL CRUISE LINES' MANGO COLADA RECIPE

Ingredients:

- 5 Ounces Bacardi 151 Rum
- 1 Package Frozen Pina Colada Mix
- 1 Package Frozen Mango Mix

Instructions:

2. With ice, combine pina colada mix and 2.5 rum. Remove from the equation.
3. With ice, combine mango mix and 2.5 Rum.
4. Pour the pina colada mix into a cocktail glass while it's still frozen. Place the mango mixture on top (keeping separated).

5. Serve with a pineapple slice and a cherry on top. Use a straw to serve.

Nutrition Facts:

Additional nutrition information is currently not available.

239.MANGO SUNRISE PIÑA COLADA
Ingredients

- 2 Ounces coconut rum
- 2 Ounces mango juice
- 2 Ounces pineapple juice
- 1 tbsp coconut cream
- 1 tbsp grenadine
- Fresh pineapple garnish

Instructions

1. In a cocktail shaker half-filled with ice, combine the coconut rum, mango, and pineapple juices. To blend and chill, give it a good shake.
2. Pour into a cocktail glass over ice.
3. Pour coconut cream in a slow, steady stream over the back of a spoon.
4. Pour the grenadine carefully over the top.

240.MANGO CASTAWAY

INGREDIENTS

- 2 cups of frozen mango
- 6 ounces aged rum (we recommend BACARDÍ™ ReservaOcho Rum)
- 4 ounces coconut rum
- 5 tbsp sweetened condensed milk
- Cocktail umbrellas, sliced fruit, flowers, maraschino cherries, and any other tiki drink decoration (optional)

PREPARATION

1. Blend mango, aged rum, coconut rum, milk, and 4 cups of ice in a blender until smooth.

2. Divide among glasses and garnish as desired.

241. BLUEBERRY-MANGO COLADA SALAD

Ingredients

- 2 cups of fresh blueberries
- Two mangos, peeled, seeded, and sliced (about 1-3/4 cups of)
- 1/4 cup of frozen piña colada mix, thawed
- 1 tbsp dark rum (optional)

Instructions

1. Combine blueberries, mangos, pia colada mix, and rum in a large mixing basin.
2. Spoon the fruit mixture evenly into four martini glasses or dessert dishes.
3. If desired, decorate with blueberries, mango slices, and thin lime slices threaded onto long toothpicks.

242. POMEGRANATE MANGO COLADA POPSICLES

Ingredients

For the Pomegranate Colada Half

- 3 Tbsp pomegranate juice
- 3/4 cup of cream of coconut (this is a pina colada cocktail syrup – see notes in the post about where to purchase)**
- 1/2 cup of vanilla greek yogurt
- 5 Ounces pomegranate seeds/arils

Instructions

1. In a blender, combine all ingredients except the pomegranate seeds and blend until smooth.
2. Distribute the pomegranate seeds evenly among the six molds.
3. Pour the coconut mixture over the seeds in the molds, about halfway, filling each one. (If you want diagonal stripes, tilt the mold at an angle.)
4. Freeze for 20 minutes before adding the sticks, which you can support with foil if required.

5. Return to the freezer for another 20 minutes, or until the mixture is excellent.

243. RECIPE: BACARDI MANGO COLADAS

- Prep Time 5 mins
- Cook Time 1 min
- Total Time 5 mins

Ingredients

330 ml coconut water – chilled

One mango – peeled (destoned and cubed – had I had more time, I would have frozen mine.)

200 ml Bacardi – chilled

A good squeeze of lime (depending on the sweetness of the mango)

spring of coriander

Touch of red chili

Instructions

1. In a blender, combine all of the ingredients and blend until smooth.
2. Serve immediately with a group of friends.
3. To get the most out of your newly embellished ring finger, serve in long-stemmed glasses.

Nutrition Facts

Recipe: Bacardi Mango Coladas

Amount Per serving servings)

Calories 311

% Daily Value*

Sodium 175mg 8%

Potassium 551mg16%

244. DIGESTIVE SMOOTHIE

Ingredients

- Two oranges
- One carrot
- Two bananas
- 1-inch piece of ginger root (about 2 cm)
- 1 cups of water (250 ml)

Instructions

1. Wash, peel, and chop the ingredients.
2. Place them in a powerful blender and blend until smooth.

245. PINEAPPLE GINGER TUMMY SOOTHING SMOOTHIE

PREP TIME5 MINUTES

TOTAL TIME5 MINUTES

Ingredients

- One frozen banana
- 1 cup of fresh pineapple
- 1/2 cup of 2%
- 1/4 cup of unsweetened almond milk, + more if necessary
- 1/2 tsp fresh grated ginger
- 1/2 tsp ground turmeric
- 2 tsp of chia seeds
- Optional: A few fresh mint leaves

Instructions

1. In a blender, combine all of the ingredients and blend until smooth. Pour into two glasses and serve right away. It makes two smoothies.

Nutrition

Servings: 2 smoothies

Serving size: 1 smoothie

Calories: 149kcal

Fat: 2.4g

Carbohydrates: 27.4g

246. SMOOTHIE FOR BLOATING

Prep Time: 5 minutes

Total Time: 5 minutes

INGREDIENTS

- 1 cup of fresh spinach
- 1/2 cucumber (peeled if desired)
- One celery stalk
- 1 cup of frozen pineapple
- 1/4 cup of papaya
- 1 tbsp fresh ginger
- 1 tbsp freshly squeezed lime juice
- 1 serving Protein Smoothie Boost

INSTRUCTIONS

2. In a blender, combine spinach, cucumber, and celery. Blend until completely smooth. If the cucumber doesn't have enough liquid, add a splash of water.
3. Combine the pineapple, papaya, ginger, and lime juice in a mixing bowl. Blend once more until the mixture is smooth.
4. Serve right away or keep refrigerated for up to 2 days in jars with tight-fitting lids.

247. DIGESTIVE AID DETOX SMOOTHIE (PINEAPPLE, GINGER & MINT)

PREP TIME 5 mins

TOTAL TIME 5 mins

INGREDIENTS

- One green banana (simply buy the greenest bananas you can find in the supermarket)
- Four dates
- 100 g frozen spinach or kale
- 100 g frozen or fresh pineapple
- 1 tsp hemp protein powder
- 1 tbsp fresh mint
- 250 ml water/green tea/dairy-free milk (use more or less depending on how thick you like your smoothie)
- 1-2 cm fresh ginger (if organic, you don't need to peel it)

INSTRUCTIONS

1. In a blender, combine all of the ingredients and blend until smooth.
2. Serve with granola and dairy-free, living yogurt; remember to chew as you eat/drink to aid digestion...

NUTRITION

Calories: 137kcalCarbohydrates: 34gProtein: 3gFat: 1gSodium: 49mgPotassium: 649mgFiber: 4gSugar: 21gVitamin A: 5328IUVitamin C: 47mgVitamin K: 241µgCalcium: 68mgFolate: 121µgIron: 2mgMagnesium: 68mg

248. HEALTHY GUT VANILLA CHAI SMOOTHIE

Prep Time: 5 minutes

Total Time: 5 minutes

INGREDIENTS

- 1 cup of steamed and frozen cauliflower*
- ¾ cup of milk of choice
- ½ cup of vanilla Greek or Icelandic-style yogurt (I like Siggi's)
- ¼ cup of rolled oats
- One date pitted
- 1 tsp chai spice
- 1 tsp vanilla extract

INSTRUCTIONS

1. Add all ingredients to a high-powered blender and blend until smooth.
2. Enjoy!

249. PREPARATION: 5 MIN

Ingredients

- 1/2 frozen banana, chopped
- 1 cup of coconut water
- One handful of spinach or rocket
- 1/2 lime, juiced
- 1/2 cucumber
- 1 tsp chia seeds
- 3-4 mint leaves
- 1/2 tsp ginger, grated
- 3-4 ice cubes

INSTRUCTIONS

1. Place all ingredients in a blender and blitz until smooth.
2. Pour into a glass and enjoy!

250. HAPPY GUT KEFIR SMOOTHIE

Prep time 10 mins

Total time 10 mins

Ingredients

- 1 cup of plain kefir (low-fat or full-fat)
- ½ cup of unsweetened vanilla almond milk (or another milk OR more kefir)
- ½ cup of frozen wild blueberries
- ½ cup of frozen diced mango (or ½ frozen banana)
- 1 tbsp flax meal
- One knob peeled ginger (about the ½-inch piece)
- One date pitted
- 2-4 tbsp parsley, about 2-4 sprigs

- 1-2 kale leaves, destemmed

Instructions

1. Mix all the ingredients in a high-powered blender and process until smooth.
2. Pour into one large or two small glasses. Enjoy!

251. FLIGHT THERAPY GREEN SMOOTHIE

Prep Time 5 minutes

Total Time 5 minutes

INGREDIENTS

- One handful of spinach (you can also use kale)
- 1/2 cup of pineapple
- 1 cup of water
- 1/4 cup of parsley tightly packed
- 1/4 cup of mint tightly packed
- 2 tbsp chia seeds
- 1/2 lime juiced
- Three ice cubes

INSTRUCTIONS

1. Toss all ingredients into a blender, and blend on high until smooth and creamy.

NUTRITION

Calories: 188kcal | Carbohydrates: 28g | Protein: 6g | Fat: 8g | Saturated Fat: 1g | Sodium: 56mg | Potassium: 502mg | Fiber: 12g | Sugar: 9g | Vitamin A: 4555IU | Vitamin C: 81mg | Calcium: 251mg | Iron: 5mg

252. TROPICAL PAPAYA PINEAPPLE KALE GREEN SMOOTHIE RECIPE

INGREDIENTS

- 2 Cup of Kale
- 1 Cup of Papaya

- 1 Cup of Pineapple
- 10 Whole Almond
- 1.5 Cup of Water
- 2 Tsp Chia Seeds

INSTRUCTIONS

2. Cut papaya and pineapple into small chunks—measure cups to get an appropriate portion.
3. Start adding papaya and pineapple to a blender
4. Add 2 cup of kale to the blender
5. Add ten whole almonds and 2 tsp chia seeds
6. Add one and half cups of water and blend until all ingredients are liquefied.

THE END